A
SACRAMENTAL
PEOPLE

Healing and Vocation

MICHAEL DRUMM *and* TOM GUNNING

TWENTY-THIRD PUBLICATIONS
BAYARD Mystic, CT 06355

Surely goodness and kindness shall follow me
all the days of my life.
Psalm 23

First published in 2000 by
The Columba Press
55a Spruce Avenue, Stillorgan Industrial Park
Blackrock, Co Dublin

North American edition, 2000
Twenty-Third Publications/ Bayard
185 Willow Street
P.O. Box 180
Mystic, CT 06355
(860) 536-2611
(800) 321-0411

ISBN:1-58595-117-X
Library of Congress Catalog Card Number: 00-134900
Printed in the U.S.A.

Contents

For Anna

Introduction

This is a companion volume to *A Sacramental People: Initiation into a Faith Community.* In that book we addressed the sacraments of initiation—Baptism, confirmation, and eucharist. This book is devoted to the sacraments of healing and vocation—anointing the sick, reconciliation, marriage, and holy orders. There is also a chapter on celebrating death.

Our goal is to contribute to the pastoral renewal of the sacraments in the life of the church. Significant numbers of people still attend sacramental gatherings and, with a little imagination and creativity, these celebrations could be an important focus for renewal in the church. Drawing on the links that exist between ritual and sacrament it is possible to renew our celebrations in such a way that they act as thresholds that can nurture faith, reflection, and an encounter with our Paschal identity.

This book is divided into four parts. Part One deals with the very nature of ritual; Part Two discusses some issues raised with regard to the sacraments of healing and the celebration of death; Part Three analyzes the two sacraments of vocation—marriage and holy orders, while Part Four provides various ideas and texts for use in the celebration of the sacraments.

The first chapter analyzes the importance of ritual in human life. This gives a foundation for a renewed understanding of the sacraments. In the succeeding chapters the reader will find a contemporary theology for each of the sacraments. We also provide ideas and texts which could be used in sacramental celebrations.

This book might be used in various ways. The first chapter could form the basis of reflection on the very nature of sacrament and ritual for a discussion group. Similarly the theology of a sacrament could be analyzed on the basis of the relevant chapter. Some might just read one chapter dealing with a particular sacrament that concerns them personally or that they could never really understand. Others might use the suggested texts for sacramental celebrations. In other words, the intention is that this book, and its companion volume, be "pastoral" in the best sense of the word—that they present a contemporary, accessible theology for each of the sacraments, that the individual reader can dip into them as he or she desires, and that they provide ideas and texts for the renewal of sacramental celebrations.

PART I

Chapter One

The Importance of Ritual

The edge and the center
One day every year a farmer asks to meet his neighbor to mend a wall that separates their farms. So the story goes in Robert Frost's poem "Mending Wall." The neighbor wonders why they should really bother, as his land is all pine and the other's is apple orchard. Yet the farmer's terse reply is that "good fences make good neighbors."

Since nomads first settled down to domesticate a piece of land we have been driven to define what is ours, to erect fences, to establish beyond doubt our boundaries. Establishing boundaries identifies the limits of our experience, our knowledge, and our ownership. We can control and structure that which is inside the boundary, and so identifying the edge determines the center, that which is structured, protected, and ordered. It is here that we must live. At the center, in the house or workplace, among family, colleagues, and friends, one finds comfort and security. It is the familiar. For some it is pensioned, mortgaged, insured life.

In archaic societies too it was at the center that structure and order were found. In the initiation ceremonies of the Kwakiutl of North America the novice is brought back to the ceremonial house after the ordeals of the forest. The novice then cries: "I am at the center of the world." Within these ceremonies of initiation there is a sense of accomplishment and ending, a sense that, in returning from the edge to the center, a goal has been achieved.

Given that the center of things is so important, an interesting phenomenon of human life is our preoccupation with the edge. On the weekend people leave the city and go to the country, the mountains, or the seashore to unwind and relax. Some even cycle off mountain ledges with parachutes, ascend precarious cliff faces, and go to endless efforts to put their lives at risk. We long for vacation time when we can leave everything behind. Yet what is so seductive about the edge, given that it is at the center that we find order and familiarity? Is it that the center cannot hold, and so periodically we need to visit the very edges or limits of experience? What can be found at boundaries that cannot be found at the center?

Frost's poem can tell us something about what happens at boundaries. It would appear that the only chance for these two farmers to meet is in the crumbling of the wall. Yet the irony is that it is only in the destruction of the wall that they meet and talk, and so it is a moment of creativity. The small crisis that befalls them every year actually maintains their relationship. Likewise those who climb rock faces or set out on the ocean in crafts better suited to small lakes create their own crises. Paradoxically these experiences become regenerative and creative. For many they provide a spiritual experience that cannot be found within structured religion. Experiences at the edge can be transformative. When one reaches the edges of one's identity and then goes beyond, nothing is ever the same again. It is as if one has gone across a threshold.

Sometimes the allure of the edge can be fashioned from a deeper need. The preoccupation with leaving the known and venturing to the boundaries of foreign territory has echoes of a heroic quest. Forcing one's identity, embracing ordeal, and crossing thresholds is an initiation of types. From present-day video games to ancestral myths, we are completely seduced by tales of leaving the ordinary and the familiar to seek boundary experiences of daring and triumph. There has been and always will be a dynamic, be it in story, drama, journey, or lived experience, of leaving the familiar and moving to the unknown—and eventually of leaving the unknown and moving back to the familiar. It is impossible to go from womb to tomb, from infancy to old age, without crossing thresholds. To experience the complete ambit of what it is to live a human life demands that we initiate ourselves continuously into the different stages of life. To do this we must leave the familiar and journey to the edge, seek thresholds, and venture across them.

Rites of passage

Arnold Van Gennep coined the term "rites of passage" in the early 1900s. His research was based on the rites that tribes and societies perform when they pass individually or collectively from one place, state, social position, or age to another. He said that in archaic societies there were always new thresholds to cross: the thresholds of summer and winter, of a season or a year, of a month or a night; the thresholds of birth, adolescence, maturity, and old age; the threshold of death and the afterlife. Just as the life of the planet must change and develop, so too the individual person must encounter different passages. One cannot remain an infant or a child forever; one must enter new identities, those of adult, mother, father, and old age. Life brings us to various edges, and we must learn how to cross them.

Concerning these transitions, primitive people gleaned a particular insight from lunar symbolism. The moon waxes and wanes, is present and absent. Somehow after it waned it seemed capable of regenerating itself. Based on lunar transitions archaic societies accepted a principle of death and rebirth in the cosmos as cosmic systems periodically renewed themselves. Yet human life too had times of transition. Just as the moon can wax and wane and regenerate itself, there is a central principle of regeneration and transformation within the biological, psychological, and spiritual aspects of human growth.

"Rites of passage" is the term we use to describe the rituals that various societies and institutions have developed to mark these important transitions in human life. Though the ritual

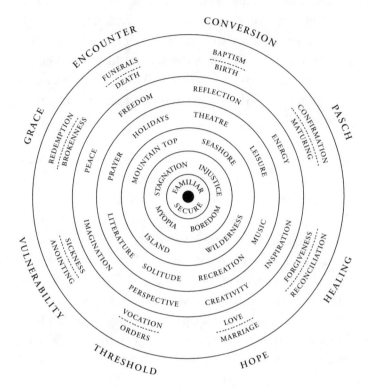

behavior of different groups varies enormously, they have one interesting characteristic in common—they share the symbolism of the edge or the threshold as a metaphor for what is happening to the individual and the group. Ritual behavior in general tends to mirror this movement away from the center and familiarity toward a threshold or edge experience. The experience of a threshold moment differs greatly from culture to culture and from one person's life to another. The threshold moment can be chosen and entered into voluntarily or it may be imposed and entered involuntarily, and so there is a distinction between the different layers of experience within ritual. Irrespective of these distinctions, what emerges is that all of life is in some way, voluntarily or involuntarily, bound up with the experience of visiting the edge and returning to the center. As we begin to examine the different layers within the process of ritual behavior, the reader will find them figuratively displayed in the diagram above. We have deliberately chosen the image of concentric circles. In the smallest circle we find ourselves at the center of life, and in the outer circles we outline the many edges and thresholds that we choose to visit or that are forced upon us.

Landscapes and seascapes

The most straightforward way to leave the familiar is to journey to the mountaintop, the forest, the seashore, or the glen. Such thresholds removed from the center, with its deadening structures and familiarity, are places of perspective and renewal. If we never leave the center of life, the place where we live and work, eat and sleep, there is a real danger of boredom and stagnation. Worse, we can begin to live in a myopic world with little sense of the injustice of so many structures. Human beings need to encounter different perspectives that might entice them away from worship of the false gods of security and familiarity.

The mountain, the seashore, the uninhabited island, the wilderness of forest and desert, have played a critical role in the history of all religions and the development of various spiritualities. In the life of the human spirit, crucial moments occur away from home. Moses was told to go to Horeb, Jonah to Nineveh, and Jacob to Haran. There is a geographical departure in all these stories. The call to the lakeshore or the seashore, the island or the brook, may not be a prophetic calling, as those above are, but it does bring fresh awareness and perspective because this is exactly what happens at thresholds.

If one were even to stand in the threshold of a room it becomes apparent there is a view of two spaces instead of one, that it is only at the threshold that one can enter or depart, that it is only here that one has a choice. There are possibilities and perspectives that can only occur at thresholds, which cannot happen at the center.

Creation is not opaque but a cipher for numinous and deep realities. To leave the urban sprawl and its stress and taste the silence or breathtaking beauty of the natural world is not necessarily about being "eco-friendly" or "new age-y." There should be no cause for embarrassment in being seduced or inspired by the stuff of nature, for it is God's creation. Much can be deciphered from the sea, the wind, and the earth for, since time began, all of creation, as St. Paul tells us, has been groaning in one great act of giving birth, and it too, like us, is waiting to be set free (see Rom 8:18–22).

Thus far we have analyzed the simplest form of ritual behavior under the heading of landscapes and seascapes. We have noted that certain places are important in the history of religious rituals. But certain times are similarly significant—dawn and dusk, the equinox and the solstice, night and darkness. So too some forms of human behavior can open the door to a heightened awareness—fasting and silence, touching and tasting, posture and odors. What all of these have in common is the capacity to bring us to a different threshold where we can see things in another way.

Dramas and journeys

There are endless roles to play in life: mother, father, teacher, priest, businessman, businesswoman. At work each day people have to be attentive to their roles and wear the appropriate mask. Teachers have to be disciplinarians, business people should be shrewd, salespeople must be sanguinely pleasant. It takes energy to play these roles, to maintain the tension between having to perform the duties of the workplace and doing what one would love to do. Yet these everyday dramas hold the center together. It is how we support industry and employment, maintain essential services, and earn a livelihood.

What is crucial to the maintenance of these roles is the ability periodically to remove oneself from the drama, to give the tensions a rest. It is vital to give time to the identity behind the mask, to wear different clothes, to laugh, to act spontaneously, to live life without a script. And life is an endless process of doing just that, of leaving the familiarized notion of self as employee or employer, child care worker or parish administrator, and journeying to the threshold. There are endless examples of these journeys: weekends away, holidays abroad, leisure activities, going to the theater, bar, or restaurant; reading the Scriptures, personal meditation, going on retreat or sabbatical; reading, writing, hobbies, and sports. All of these offer the possibility of leaving our masks aside for a while and encountering others, the planet, life, and maybe even God in a different way.

Whether one experiences landscapes or seascapes, dramas or journeys, one cannot but be seduced by the threshold. Look at what can happen there: freedom and possibility, change and regeneration, transformation and meaningful relationships. The journey to the threshold can be likened to revisiting the edges of Eden, from whence we were once cast. Within the script and security of the familiar there can be a deep restlessness, a sense of paradise lost, that life can be better, that the center can be more true, more meaningful. Without a doubt, a paradise of sorts is found in some of these leisure activities.

The threshold is the place of meaningful encounter because those who meet there are truly themselves. Just like Frost's experience of mending the wall, thresholds can become the location of creativity in life. There is no hidden agenda forced by the demands of productivity. Likewise, being alone and choos-

ing to be away from the crowd can provide moments of genuine encounter with the deeper realities of life. In writing or
meditation, solitude or prayer, one looks inside as into a well,
going down for the good stuff, where the flame of clarity and
truth can enlighten the darkness of silence and solitude.

In all of this there is one necessary and vital act, that of separation. One cannot experience what happens at the threshold
unless one first separates from the familiar or one journeys in
some way toward the edge. This can include a geographical
movement, a change of setting, of clothes, or of focus. Often in
life this journey of separation is longed for, planned and saved
for, yet there is a darker side to the threshold. Thus far we have
considered the examples of times when we voluntarily move
to the edge and away from what is common and banal.
However, there are times in life when one is forced to the edge,
when the movement is involuntary.

A fruitful darkness

There are experiences in life that are harsh and oftentimes unwelcome. To be forced away from the center is more often than
not a chaotic experience. And life does this to us at times.
Bereavement is the outstanding example. When we lose someone close, a familiar face and voice is missing from the home:
nothing can be the same again. Familiarity has disappeared.
Tragedy can strike in many guises and forms—financial, social, medical. A crisis can occur at any stage in life, particularly
in times of transition or passage when we are forced to leave
something behind. Children must leave dependence to become independent adults. All of us at some time have to let go
of the idea that we are still young, just as surely as we must accept the idea that we have now become old. Life is a process of
letting go, of moving from one threshold to another.
Unwelcome as tragedy is, it needn't always be pure darkness.
Painful separations can often precede creative breakthroughs.

How many times have we heard of the family difficulty that brought everyone together, or the personal crisis that brought someone out of self-centeredness and egotism to become more caring and altruistic? How many times has crisis deepened and made genuine our relationships, how many times has it brought us closer to God? One can argue that it is only in crisis and chaos, within the thresholds of sickness, loss, and hurt, that the most meaningful experiences emerge in life—forgiveness, healing, altruism, growth, and transformation.

Let us view life as a process of being brought involuntarily to different threshold moments. From the moment we are born we are pushed from our mother's womb into a world of love and loss, hope and despair, expectation and promise, life and death. It is something we never requested; we are simply landed into life. We grow to become children, yet as the years progress it is demanded of us that we mature. We must separate ourselves from childhood ways, sacrificing dependency and irresponsibility for commitment and duty. All through life we will suffer some form of heartbreak, pain, loss, and hurt. Our relationships will experience rupture through forgetfulness, infidelity, and selfishness. Hurt spawns bitterness and regret, yet these realities can lead us toward thresholds of forgiveness and reconciliation.

Life pushes us in other directions as well. Nobody can design or plan love, it just happens, and the happiness that it creates can sustain a lifetime of sacrifice and commitment. Others experience a desire to live life according to a different set of values. These are called to ordained ministry or religious life through which they craft their own interpretation of discipleship. Finally, sickness and death await the strongest and fittest of us all. All living things must grow feeble as the strength and vigor of life give way to the unrelenting process of time. These are the thresholds that we must cross if we are to live truly human lives. Whether we like it or not we will be brought to these places.

Significantly, Christian tradition has made sacraments of these moments. Baptism initiates a person into the church and is often celebrated soon after birth, while confirmation, when it is celebrated in late childhood or early adolescence, marks a threshold on the road to maturity. The sacrament of reconciliation challenges us to live the reality of Christian forgiveness. Marriage and holy orders are the sacraments of commitment and vocation, while the sacrament of the sick gives strength to those who are ill or dying. It is the most basic insight of Christian belief that we live in a broken, fragile, and sinful world. Redemption is to be found not by turning one's back on the sad difficulties of life but, like Christ himself, by embracing the realities that confront us.

Interestingly, no single threshold moment in life relates directly to the Eucharist. But look at the diagram on page 5. In order to keep the center renewed, creative, just, and meaningful, it becomes the work of life to continually offer ourselves to the transformative power of thresholds, to separate, to find new perspectives. In the Eucharist it is work like this that we bring to the altar. The key thresholds in life that we celebrate in many of the sacraments can often be extremely sacrificial in nature, be that birth or maturing, commitment or letting go. Yet the gifts of bread and wine symbolize the offering and sacrifice that we make continuously throughout our lives. Just as we can be rent apart within the act of self-giving, so too the bread is broken, the grapes are crushed. We offer our own self-sacrifice, we offer the work of our human hands.

So far we have examined the ritual process and the rhythm of leaving the center, being renewed and returning again. Sometimes the rhythm back and forth is voluntary, sometimes involuntary, but there is little doubt that significant change can take place: from childhood to maturity, bitterness to reconciliation, self-sufficiency to love, life to death. Yet taken at

whatever level, one truth emerges, and it is this: without ritual
the center cannot hold, for there is no transition or change, no
genuine relationships. Without ritual I go nowhere, I see nothing new, and I do it alone.

At the center

If structure, order, and the familiar define the center, then
within the church we have definite structures and an ordered
and familiar way of going about the business of being a Christian
people. Dioceses and parishes are organized in a very structured way, and there is a particular order and familiarity to the
liturgical year and our celebration of the sacraments. Our
churches are often constructed with high steeples and thick
pillars, suggesting the proximity and strength of our link with
the divine. There is a comforting steadfastness and security
about them. Within all these structures, faith and meaning,
understanding and tradition can persevere and endure. All of
this is as it should be, and it is how all religions endure the
persecutions of time. This is the nature of the center. But we
need to be aware that the center cannot hold unless it is periodically immersed in the experience of the threshold and the
edge.

A church bereft of an experience of the threshold could become prone to stagnation and myopia. Accepted understandings
or interpretations would not be revisited, and so the church
could be condemned as irrelevant by a new generation. But
there is a spirit within the church that frowns upon such an
understanding of things. There is something unsettling and
restless at the heart of Christianity.

After his baptism, Jesus is sent into the wilderness by the
Spirit. And of this same Spirit John tells us: "The wind blows
wherever it pleases; you hear its sound, but you cannot tell
where it comes from or where it is going. That is how it is with

all who are born of the Spirit" (Jn 3:8). This is not the Spirit of stagnation or conservatism, but the Spirit of the threshold, of critique and imagination, of change and possibility. Strangely, and in keeping with what we know of thresholds, it is also the Spirit of chaos. In the book of Genesis we read that at the moment of creation there was a formless void, there was darkness over the deep, and God's Spirit hovered over the water (Gen 1:2). There was chaos, yet this is where God's Spirit was to be found, and this is also true of human life. Creation is to be found in chaos, in the fruitful darkness of genesis.

The church community that is bold enough to visit the uncertainty of the edge may have to experience the darkness of disorientation and the confusion of losing established patterns of understanding and doing. But this group will open itself to the possibility of true community and closer relationships. It will experience possibility and change. It will be a freer community, capable of embracing self-critique. In short, it will be a community that can realign itself to discipleship and gospel values. It will be a community based on the Spirit of creation and transformation.

Two thousand years ago Jesus preached the dawning reign of God. His message was anti-fashion, unconventional, and disturbing. The reign of God runs contrary to prevailing values and opinions, as attested to in the many parables of Jesus. They seem designed to disrupt our cozy views. In his first letter to the Corinthians, St. Paul tells us that God's foolishness is wiser than human wisdom, God's weakness stronger than human strength (1 Cor 1:25). That God sees things differently than we do seems woven into the very fabric of Judaism and Christianity. For those who follow God's word there is serious disruption. Moses was sent to Horeb, Jacob to Haran, and Jesus to the wilderness. That God disturbs comfort and inertia are threads that run through the fabric of divine revelation throughout history.

Jesus lived his life on the edge, at the threshold. Why? Because that is where the divine can be encountered, and Jesus, being the fullness of divinity present in humanity, invites us into the very life of God. But this is a difficult path because we discover that true community is found in poverty and disruption, that discipleship will push us to the edge, and that little that really matters is the way it appears to be. Life appears almost as a negative of itself, the shadows become light, and the brightness is shaded. Carl Jung once remarked that if a friend were to inform him of great news of promotion or financial gain Jung would commiserate. However, if the friend told him that some crisis had befallen him Jung would suggest that they crack open champagne. That we can hope in darkness is almost like a beatitude.

When we speak of ritual we refer to that dynamic in life of leaving the familiar, the banal, to savor something nearer the edges of experience. Life will bring us to these places or we may choose to go there voluntarily. It is the task of the local church community to ensure, at least on certain occasions, that its sacramental celebrations are indeed encounters with life on the edge. Congregating to hear the unconventional wisdom of the gospels, to savor the rich symbolism of Catholicism, and to participate in the very life of God in the Eucharist—these have the potential to be threshold moments. When we gather to celebrate Christianity we contest and challenge the isolation and stifling privacy of modern life, because at the center of urban or city life this type of activity is fast becoming unfashionable. Our purpose now is to examine ways in which we can strengthen and reinvigorate the sacramental life of a Christian community. The following pointers, which include the insights that we have just gleaned from our study of ritual, might give a renewed focus to the sacraments.

Word and symbol

Every day we use words and language to communicate ideas, feelings, and information. Words serve us well at a particular level, yet they begin to flounder when we try to speak about deeper realities, stronger emotions, or the numinous. Poetry and music have the ability to find a deeper echo in our minds and hearts. Eventually, however, language must give way to other forms of symbolic communication. When meaning is no longer held, or begins to lose its moorings in language, it is anchored again in symbol. And when meaning begins to lose its moorings in symbol, it is anchored again in the word. In death we can often find no words to comfort because language simply can't express grief, and so we embrace. In love, two lovers may talk forever but their truest feelings will find expression in a kiss or the exchange of rings. If one were to really try to explain the effects of love or death, words would flounder, and so language takes on symbolic expression. Symbols are born from language and story.

Symbols lose their meaning if divorced from the story that originally gave them expression. Wedding rings mean little if the couple who wear them are no longer in love. In this instance, the only way for the rings to mean something again is for the couple to revisit and rediscover the story of what attracted them together in the first place. Here a symbol desperately needs to be reborn again out of the story that first gave it life. If we are presented with a symbol that evokes no memory, feeling, or experience, then it is meaningless because we can't relate it to a story.

When we apply the above insights to our celebration of the sacraments, our attention should focus on how closely we align our use of symbols to the story from whence they originated. It becomes a means of presenting them more effectively. So, for example, a community must question how effectively it presents water as a symbol. What is so special about bread and wine? Why did Jesus choose to share his presence with us in a meal? Why do we light candles? What is so significant about light and dark? When we answer these questions we unify word and symbol, story and expression. It is crucial to be aware of the fact that symbols allow us access to the deepest of life's realities, feelings, and insights way beyond the realm of language. Therefore to stifle the use of our Christian symbols either through minimalism or indifference is to deny a community some of its most profound experiences.

Awakening a sense of the edge/threshold in sacramental celebrations

If I want to move to the threshold of a room I must first leave it. To move from the familiarity of the center toward the edge, one must encounter something that is strange or do something unfamiliar. This is the nature of separation because the strange or the inexplicable awakens reflection. Separation perplexes and creates questions. It awakens.

There are many ways of creating separation, whether in the context of the sacraments themselves or in the context of celebrating our faith. Perhaps the easiest way to create separation is by going somewhere unfamiliar. Mountains, rivers, lakes, seashores, forests, ruins, or wells can all be places of reflection and renewal. Deserts and islands can be more unfamiliar and therefore more liminal locations. It has always been part of the heritage of any religion that there are sacred places where one can encounter the divine. The Scriptures are full of such examples.

Just as there are sacred places, there have always been sacred times. Our forebears were much more in tune with the movements of the sun and moon. The solstices and equinoxes were times set apart for special activities. The movement of the liturgical year through the different seasons is not arbitrary, and the linking of Easter with spring accentuates the value of the story of Passover. These are sacred times, and they set us apart, making us particularly conscious of some aspect of our Christian story. We normally celebrate our sacraments in daylight or electric light. Yet imagine in darkness the sense of separation that could be evoked by simply gathering together in candlelight. So too, dawn and dusk are threshold moments that witness the unfolding of darkness and light. The symbolic value of light and dark is immense and can be easily woven into the rich tapestry of life with its sadness and joy, its hope and despair.

Separation can also be created through the senses. We interpret our world continuously through our senses and we can immediately detect an unfamiliar sight, sound, touch, taste, or smell. The sacraments have always seduced our senses, and the church has long known how effectively it can communicate its message in this way. Just look at taste. Water, wine, honey, milk, vinegar, all have a Christian symbolic value as do salt, lamb, bread, oil, and herbs. As church attendance declines it would appear that there is an increase in the purchase of scented oils and candles. Yet our sacraments could be replete with candles, and the fragrance of balsam and incense. Even outside of the Christian story, scents, oils, and candles have deep symbolic value, and people will always be drawn to them. Remember that all of creation is groaning, waiting to be set free, and so we should use the things of the earth to celebrate our redemption.

We have visited the many layers of ritual in life. Without a doubt, ritual is vital to the well-being of the individual and society. It is the source of change, critique, and regeneration. We examined the different layers and types of threshold moments that we can encounter. Those nearest the center of life are not so unfamiliar, like seascapes and journeys. We noticed however that the most transforming experiences in life were in ordeal, tragic moments of loss and crisis, or at the threshold moments that are celebrated in the sacraments. These experiences are furthest from the center of life, and their unfamiliarity disturbs greatly. An experience of tragedy or passage cuts so finely that its effects are always buried deep.

Conclusion

The center of life is characterized by habit and familiarity. It is comfortable and secure but nothing significant happens here; habit is anathema to imagination and change. Unfortunately the sacraments can often be experienced more at the center of life than at the edge. Many will say that Mass can become a mere habit or routine, that it is tedious and repetitive. Others will condemn baptism as being ineffectual, no more than a social custom. And yet nothing could be further from the truth. The sacraments do not point to the center but instead they are doors opening out onto the edge of life. God is not encountered in a life enslaved to routine, but instead in the vulnerability of pain and loss and in the openness of a cry that comes from deep within. The reality is that grace and hope can only be encountered when we are pushed to the outer edges of life's experience.

The sacraments receive their life from the events of Easter, and consequently they are defined by experiences that are truly paschal. At Easter we witness a humanity that knows isolation, betrayal, and brokenness. Yet in spite of incomprehensible suffering and loss, at the empty tomb we find hope and healing. In the upper room there is doubt and despair, yet ultimately transformation and conversion. Those who see their lives woven into the narrative of Pasch will also see their lives in the bread that is broken and the wine that is given. At times they will have been overcome by the waters of the Jordan and assuaged by the oils of gladness and by the presence of Christ. The story of a sacramental people is a story of a people brought to the edge and to places where they would rather not go. Yet these are the significant moments of life; this is the place of healing. This is Easter.

PART II

Sacraments of Healing

In this part of the book we will study the two sacraments of healing—anointing the sick and reconciliation. At their most intense these sacraments can truly be encounters with life on the edge. However, they often fail to make such an impact on the lives of the participants and their communities. We also devote a chapter to the ultimate human experience that is the threshold of death.

Chapter Two

Anointing the Sick

The ministry of Jesus

Almost two thousand years ago Jesus of Nazareth spoke of the reign of God as healing for the sick, hearing for the deaf, new sight for the blind, freedom for prisoners, good news for the poor. Before we can really appreciate the meaning of healing, hearing, new sight, freedom, and good news, we need to become aware of the realities of sickness, deafness, blindness, captivity, and poverty. When we look honestly at ourselves we discover that we are the sick, the deaf, the blind, the captive, the poor, and not just in some abstract metaphorical sense but in the physical, psychological, and spiritual realities of our lives. Only when we immerse ourselves in these human experiences can we discover who Jesus really was, for his ministry was all about lifting burdens. Whether the burdens were created by a scrupulously strict religious sensibility or blind obedience or political corruption or grinding poverty or sickness or lack of self-esteem or pride or prejudice, the result was the same: people were in need of healing. The meaning of the miracle stories in the gospels is not that Jesus was some sort of esoteric magician who could solve all of life's most inscrutable problems, but rather that he was one who brought healing and hope into the most abject human situations.

The world is full of evil. Unless one lives a completely blinkered, egocentric existence, the pain of human experience is all too obvious to see. In facing this reality we can turn our backs in despair or throw our hands in the air at the futility of human life. But the call of Christian discipleship demands otherwise. It demands that we always seek to lift the burden. Whether this means helping people to stand up and walk on their own, or exorcising their fear of the unknown, or expanding their minds through education, or feeding them when they are too weak to feed themselves, or opening their eyes to the reality of life, or challenging them to let go of hurts and prejudice, or liberating those who are unjustly oppressed, or introducing them to ever greater horizons of transcendence and beauty, or unsealing their ears to hear the divine echo in their hearts, or unleashing their hope for the future, or sowing the seeds of eternal life, the healing ministry of Jesus is continued as "the blind see again, the lame walk, lepers are cleansed, and the deaf hear, the dead are raised to life, the good news is proclaimed to the poor" (Lk 7:22). Once a person receives the gift of healing then the possibility arises of moving on without the crutch or the grudge or the closed mind, while the future is no longer dictated by forces outside the individual but becomes an invitation to personal fulfillment.

Of all the questions raised by the existence of evil and suffering in our world, none is greater than this—why do the innocent suffer? This is the great question posed to all religious belief. Nothing so subverts our faith in humanity, in God, in the future. Nobody can explain life's most terrible tragedies. In the tradition of the Jewish prophets, of Job and of Jesus himself, we are asked to do our best to alleviate suffering, not to acquiesce in unjust structures that condemn people to endless pain. We are asked to hope against hope and, in the end, to surrender to a mystery greater than ourselves. We must not speak a pathetic message of joy and luck to a sad and broken world. Rather we must face the difficulties with whatever grace and dignity we can muster. Christian tradition tells us that suffering can be redemptive. It is hard to really believe this. Maybe the only way to discover what it could mean is to reflect on the reality of healing in our lives.

Healing

It is unquestionably true to say that the most important dimension of Christian discipleship is healing. The church exists not primarily to get bigger or more efficient in its work but to bring healing and hope into a broken world. All members of the church are asked to participate in this task of helping those who are blinded by prejudice or lame through addiction or deaf to others or dumb in bereavement or crippled by illness or imprisoned by history. The list of burdens goes on and on. In Jesus' ministry healing came through the spoken word and the laying on of hands. The human words of kindness, compassion, and justice can indeed heal, but words can also wreak havoc in their bitterness, apathy, and prejudice. The word of healing will often be a word of honesty where we face up to the reality of human situations. Sometimes it will be a word of forgiveness that sets people free to move onward. On other occasions it will be a word of comfort, often spoken in tears and heartbreak. But this word is always worth speaking, even when we might feel that it is useless or empty, because it is clear from the ministry of Jesus that the word can heal.

Jesus also laid his hands on those who suffered. We should not underestimate the significance of human touch. At times it speaks more loudly than words and can give affirmation and strength to those who are in need. To be a source of healing, the word and the laying on of hands demand faith. Obviously from a purely human point of view they can appear empty and meaningless. But when given and received in faith they can be a source of healing. One should note here that we are talking about healing rather than cure. Many people have been cured who were never healed, and many who were healed were never cured.

Christians should interpret suffering and human limitation in the light of the death and resurrection of Christ. We need to look again at the meaning of sickness, addictions, psychiatric breakdowns, death, and bereavement. From a Christian perspective one cannot just view these realities as disasters, but rather as part of the paschal mystery of Christ in which we all share. As we described in chapter one, these are truly thresholds in life that we would prefer to avoid, but which inevitably come our way. Even though we could never welcome these experiences, our Christian faith asks us truly to face up to them, for only by crossing these thresholds can we move on. Christianity does not provide escape hatches from life's problems but it demands that we encounter the true meaning of redemption at the very edges of our experience. This goes very much against the dominant cultural values of western societies today where human limitation in all its forms—sickness, disability, addiction, death—is frowned upon and ignored, hoping that it will go away. But Christians should take a counter-cultural approach in the embrace of human limitation and failure as the key to understanding who we are and what our destiny is.

The sacrament of anointing the sick

No sacrament is more misunderstood than this one. In large part this is due to its complex history. The use of oil for comforting and healing the sick was common in Middle Eastern cultures. This theme is taken up in a famous passage in the Letter of James: "Are any among you sick? They should call for the elders of the church and have them pray over them, anointing them with oil in the name of the Lord. The prayer of faith will save the sick and the Lord will raise them up; and anyone who has committed sins will be forgiven" (Jas 5:14–15). Note that this text refers to sick people rather than to those who are dying. In the early centuries of the church there is some evidence of sick people being anointed. This was intended to strengthen them in their physical or psychological illness rather than having some invisible spiritual effect or anticipating their deaths.

Toward the end of the first millennium, anointing the sick became associated with the sacrament of penance. The latter was normally postponed until near one's death, and so anointing also became associated with death. Thus it came to be called "extreme unction," the rite associated with the last unction or breath of life. As this understanding became dominant it was felt that one could only receive the sacrament in danger of death, and questions were raised over whether it might only be received once. Between the Council of Trent and the Second Vatican Council there was a renewed emphasis on this being a sacrament for the sick as well as for the dying, but there is little doubt that in the popular mind being anointed by a priest was associated with nearness to death.

Vatican II introduced important reforms with regard to this sacrament. Most notably it changed its name from "extreme unction" or "the last rites" to "the anointing of the sick." As with all the sacraments it emphasized the importance of faith, the word, and the community. The proper context for the celebration of the sacrament is communal; it must always include a reflection on the word of God, and it should affirm and nourish faith. Three forms of the rite are now commonplace. There is a ritual to be celebrated with those who are sick, a distinct rite for those who are dying, and a third form where the sacrament is associated with penance and the giving of holy communion.

The problem with the reforms is that they have made little, if any, impact on the popular mind of many ordinary Catholics. Anointing is often still perceived to be associated with imminent death. Let's turn our attention to this issue first. There are three sacraments linked to the death of a Christian—penance, anointing, and Eucharist (called viaticum when received by someone close to death). The final sacrament is Eucharist and not anointing. This point is all important. The most significant sacrament of all seven is the Eucharist; participation in it is the fullest expression of Catholic faith, and it draws believers into the heart of the mystery of the death and resurrection of Christ. The most important journey any human being ever makes is across the threshold of life into the mystery of death, and it is only right, if the opportunity arises (as clearly it doesn't in sudden death), to associate this passage with the Eucharist by partaking of the body of Christ. If this renewed theology is to be communicated to people in general, then we need to set the anointing of the sick in a broader context.

This is a difficult task. No sacrament was in more need of reform in the light of Vatican II because it had tended to be always celebrated in a one-to-one context (priest and the very ill person) and often in a very mechanistic manner (almost akin to a medical intervention) due to the urgency of the situation. If we are to change people's perception of the sacrament, then pastors and others need to take heed of the following issues.

Care of the sick and the old

One of the main intentions of the renewed rites after Vatican II was to move us away from any mechanistic understanding of the sacraments. With regard to the anointing of the sick, this demands a change in our approach to the sacrament. Illness and old age are not disasters waiting to befall us, they are part of our paschal destiny. Nor are they purely physical realities marking our human demise; for Christians, they are part of our journey toward divine fulfillment. As such they must be integrated into the life of the local Christian community. Everything from depression and addiction to cancer and cardiac problems to terrible results of violence and car accidents, and much more besides, exists in our communities. We must foster a sense of the whole community being responsible for those of its members who suffer greatly. There is a real temptation for the sick and the old to withdraw into lonely isolation. The Christian community must reach out to bring healing into the brokenness of serious illness and old age. Earlier we noted that healing in the ministry of Jesus was linked to the word and the laying on of hands.

In the case of those who are being cared for at home, the community, or some subsection of it, should gather to speak this word and lay hands on the sick person. The ideal context for doing this is during a celebration of the Eucharist. Such a gathering should not be postponed until the sick or elderly person is too ill or feeble to play any part. During the Mass a relative or friend might speak words of Christian consolation and hope. The priest should invite all to pray for healing as he anoints the person; he might invite those present to link hands or to hold their hands aloft as he lays hands on the sick person. Remember that all of this is done in faith. We should not perceive illness or old age as purely physical realities; they are much more. Christians pray for healing not only at a physical level but also at a psychological and spiritual depth that goes beyond what the eye can see. Celebrating the sacrament of the anointing of the sick in the presence of the community of family, friends, and neighbors awakens all present to the reality of limitation and frailty in our lives. If the sacrament is postponed until near death it is unlikely that the community can be present; the sick person might not even be aware of what is happening, and it will probably take place in a hospital. Priests, or others who must decide, should not be over-scrupulous in determining who should be anointed or the number of times that an individual should partake in the sacrament.

Many parishes now provide occasions when the sick and elderly can come together to celebrate the Eucharist and be anointed. One Sunday in the year might be set aside for the celebration of anointing within the usual Masses on that day. A parishioner who has endured a serious illness might speak of his or her experience in the light of the gospel. Again this has the advantage of integrating the seriously ill and the elderly into the life of the community as a whole. It will also continue the process of alerting believers to the fact that our faith is centered on Easter; Christianity is not just a human philosophy that one should be good to one's neighbor—it is the revelation that life and death are inseparable and that only through death will new life be born.

Care of the dying

In the sacramental life of the church the pastoral care of the dying revolves around Eucharist, reconciliation, and anointing. We badly need to rediscover the ancient tradition of the church that the food for the final journey (viaticum) is the Eucharist. This is the last sacrament. Many people close to death naturally desire to receive absolution and to be anointed. When a priest is called to minister to someone close to death his first concern should be to carry the Eucharist to this person. The opportunity for absolution might or might not provide itself. In this context, anointing is the least significant of the three sacraments. Of course practicalities dictate what can actually be done.

Ideally, viaticum should be received during a celebration of the Eucharist. Commonly this will not be possible. The rite for reception outside Mass is as follows:

> Greeting
> Sprinkling with holy water
> Penitential rite
>
> Reading
> Homily
> Baptismal profession of faith
> Litany

> Lord's prayer
> Communion as viaticum
> Silent prayer
> Concluding prayer
>
> Blessing
> Sign of peace

The intention is that this rite be celebrated with family and friends. There is a notable emphasis on the significance of baptism at this time. During the celebration of baptism, even that of a child, the church notes that the individual is born to die. It is apt then that as death approaches all present recall the meaning of baptism, when we were immersed in the paschal mystery of the death and resurrection of Christ. Communion may be received under both kinds during this ritual, though the very ill person may only be able to receive under the form of wine. The Eucharist is administered to the sick person with the following words proper to viaticum: "May the Lord protect you and lead you to eternal life." It is very appropriate that the ritual closes with the sign of peace. The participants should not be shy about using song and music at a time like this, when these heightened forms of human expression can speak louder than the spoken word. If the very ill linger for some time after having received viaticum then communion should be brought to them regularly for the rest of their time among us.

Particular issues raised in hospital ministry

Because of modern developments in medical science and the exponential growth in healthcare provision, much pastoral care of the sick and the dying is now hospital based. This leads to difficulties particularly with regard to the provision of the sacraments. One principle should be absolutely clear—the ordinary context for the celebration of the sacraments is the parish, and this is as true of the anointing of the sick as it is for any of the other sacraments. The problem with celebrating the sacraments in the hospital context, particularly the rite of anointing, is that it can be subject to gross misinterpretation. It is easy for participants and onlookers alike to perceive the priest's action in this sacrament as something akin to a medical intervention. It is nothing of the sort. It is an act of communal worship on the part of Christian believers who intercede for healing in the lives of those beset by illness and infirmity. It should never be perceived as an action on the spiritual plane attempting to achieve much the same results as medical action on the human level in terms of cure or the lessening of pain. There is no similarity between medical intervention and sacramental celebration; the former belongs to the realm of human science, the latter is based on faith and hope in God's word.

Those involved in the pastoral care of the sick in hospitals should take certain steps to foster a deeper understanding of the meaning of sacramental celebrations in their work. In some hospitals this might demand that they call into question certain policies and traditions that, to put it mildly, have little to do with a proper understanding of the sacraments. Such steps should include the following.

a) The provision of a space, even if it is small, where the sacraments might be celebrated. While the sacraments will commonly be provided at the bedside, there should be regular occasions to celebrate them in a context that gives more space and time to explore the full meaning of the action. Such oratories or churches might also provide a space for reflection and prayer in a busy hospital situation.

b) Clear efforts to awaken everyone to the fact that the last sacrament of the church is viaticum. Given that many of those involved in hospital ministry are now non-ordained, this emphasis is particularly important. Only ordained priests and bishops can administer the anointing of the sick. If people per-

ceive the latter to be the last sacrament of the church then a
priest will have to be called even if he is not the member of a
pastoral care team who has been ministering to the particular
person. Emphasizing viaticum as the last sacrament would
take away this preoccupation with anointing close to the time
of death.

c) Stopping the abuse of anointing those who have already
died. The sacraments are the sacraments of the living, not of
the dead. When a person dies we commend him or her to
God's care. Many priests feel that they should anoint corpses
in order to console the bereaved. In doing so they are reinforc-
ing the misinterpretation of the sacrament in the lives of the
faithful. It suggests a mechanistic intervention that can somehow influence the salvation of the individual who has died.
There are many things that might be done by a priest or another minister instead of this. The corpse could be blessed with
holy water; all present might be invited to trace the sign of the
cross on the one who has died (as happens in baptism); and
the group should be led in prayers that are familiar and comforting.

Conclusion

Through its rituals that deal with the sick, the infirm, and the
dying, the church makes clear that far from running away
from these realities Christians want to lay hands and anoint, to
speak the words of healing and to touch the wounds of life.
From the perspective of Christian belief the beautiful body is
not the one found on television commercials or magazine cov-
ers but rather it is the broken body in need of healing and
strength.

In John's gospel we read the famous story of Thomas, who
would not believe in the resurrection of Jesus unless he could
put his hand and fingers into the wounds of his body. To have
faith in the resurrection is to put one's hands into the wounds

of life and still be able to believe and hope. In the First Letter of Peter we read that "through his wounds you have been healed." It is only through becoming aware of our woundedness that we can ever know what healing really is.

Chapter Three

Reconciliation

Nothing is more important in life than reconciliation. The most basic insight of Christian belief is that we live in a human world characterized by sin and failure. As a result relationships are ruptured, people say and do terrible things to one another, hatred and vengeance can consume our lives, jealousy and egoism can rule our hearts. In the midst of such sad failure Christian faith speaks of forgiveness and reconciliation. One should be careful in speaking of these realities, because words can be cheap but forgiveness and reconciliation are notoriously difficult.

Most adults can recall a time when they felt genuinely hurt by another person or an institution or a system. Presuming that they were truly injured, and that they didn't just want to take offense, what does it mean to say that they might forgive and be reconciled? At a human level, there are several arguments for attempting reconciliation. If one continues to bear the hurt then the offender dominates one's life and, as the victim, one's suffering endures. We often speak about forgiving and forgetting. If one can actually forget what happened so much the better because one can then move on. The problem with this is that most serious problems cannot simply be forgotten. In fact, such forgetfulness tends to be repression rather than reconciliation, and so the same problem emerges later in life. One might try to clear the air through some honest dialogue. But this doesn't change the fact that the victim is the victim and the offender is the offender. When all else fails one can turn to the law courts to seek redress for the harm caused. But the law can be a blunt instrument, and justice is not always done. From a human point of view, it is probably true to say that the best hope is that the problem will simply go away so that one can get on with one's life.

The Christian perspective on these realities is different. It is constructed on the premise that all of us are sinners, that none of us lives without spot or stain, that all of us would be found guilty before a heavenly tribunal. This is why St. Paul speaks about the law as condemning us. The religious law of the Jews (the torah) was meant to be liberating; through living a disciplined life in accord with the prescriptions of the law the believer would be freed from so much that is coarse and superficial in the world. But instead of being liberating, the law became a burden, and, measured against it, human beings were condemned by it. Maybe the best example of how something intended to be liberating can become oppressive is the command to keep the sabbath holy. What could be more liberating than the command to stop working, to take time off and look at the world in a different way, to be with loved ones in worshipping God and giving thanks? But the keeping of the sabbath itself became a great burden as endless minutiae had to be observed. That we could turn such a liberating command into an oppressive burden is sufficient proof that we need to be saved. Add to this our great difficulty in truly being reconciled and forgiving, and it becomes clear that we are in serious need of help. That is why the early Christians said that Christ saved us from our sins. Paul said that we are justified by faith.

The language of justification sounds strange to modern ears but it is central to New Testament theology. What does the term mean? We often speak of the need to justify ourselves or our arguments. Paul's claim is that none of us can justify ourselves before God, and that in justice we should be condemned for our failures. But the good news is that God has reconciled us in Christ, that the guilty have been acquitted, that sin has been forgiven. As a result we can be reconciled with one another, for we know the depth of our own sinfulness. At a human level, we seek to justify ourselves, to stand our ground and to seek recompense when we are harmed. But for those who believe in Christ there is a new creation founded on the forgiving love of God revealed on the cross. The basic Christian message is the reconciliation of human persons with God through Jesus of Nazareth. The great biblical testimony to this is found in the second letter to the Corinthians.

> For anyone who is in Christ there is a new creation; the old creation has gone, and now the new one is here. It is all God's work. It was God who reconciled us to himself through Christ and gave us the work of handing on this reconciliation. In other words, God in Christ was reconciling the world to himself, not holding men's faults against them, and he has entrusted to us the news that they are reconciled. So we are ambassadors for Christ; it is as though God were appealing through us, and the appeal that we make in Christ's name is: be reconciled to God. For our sake God made the sinless one into sin, so that in him we might become the goodness of God. (2 Cor 5:17–21)

The early believers thought that after this act of reconciliation those who were part of the new creation would not sin again. The two great rituals of this new community were baptism and the breaking of bread. Through baptism believers were washed clean in the blood of the lamb and, in the eucharistic gathering, this new creation was celebrated and renewed. Right down to today the most important sacraments of reconciliation are baptism and Eucharist. That is why at every celebration of baptism we acknowledge the need for the individual to be saved from sin and why the Eucharist contains a penitential rite.

A distinct sacrament

The first believers thought that, after baptism, they would never sin again. For if they did, that would surely nullify the meaning of their baptism. But believers did sin and sinned grievously. This posed serious questions about the very nature of Christian belief. Was baptism truly efficacious in taking sin away? If someone sinned seriously would that person have to be baptized again? Should the community expel such sinners given that their behavior was scandalous to the faith of sincere believers? It was in coming to terms with these pastoral concerns that the church developed a distinct sacrament to deal with the reconciliation of those who had already been baptized.

The church decided early on that baptism could never be repeated. To do so would be to call into question the efficacy of what God had done in Christ. But the problem of what to do with the sinner remained. For lesser offenses penitential exercises like fasting or almsgiving might suffice but the serious sins of murder, apostasy, and adultery demanded something more. This led the church to accept the idea of excommunication, which meant (and still means today) that a member of the community is excluded from the Eucharist. It does not mean, and never meant, that baptism has been revoked or nullified. Excommunication was a very public act, and the sinner could only be readmitted to the eucharistic table after clear repentance and penance. This group of sinners was called "the order of penitents." The nature of reconciliation in the early church was communal and public. The sin injured the life of the community, and so the repentance and penance would have to be public. But that was to change.

The early Irish church had developed a distinct form of penance based on the monastic structure that dominated on the island. The system evolved from monks accusing themselves of even small transgressions and then being levied with

the appropriate penance. This developed into a "private" form
of penance where the penitents confessed their sins to the
priest, who gave them the penance set out for the particular
offense. This model of reconciliation was spread all over
Europe by Irish missionaries in the seventh and eighth centuries. Over succeeding centuries this form of the sacrament became dominant. The confession of one's sin to a priest became
the mark of the rite, while the elements of conversion and
penance began to fade. Thus the sacrament came to be known
as "confession." In time the anonymity and secrecy of confession were emphasized, and this led to the introduction of con-
fessionals in churches in the sixteenth century. The Protestant
Reformers of that same century rejected the sacrament of confession because they believed that it undermined the true meaning of salvation in Christ. Martin Luther used to attend the
sacrament almost daily but he came to reject it as having more
to do with human scrupulosity than faith in Christ. In the
counter-reformation Catholic church frequency of attendance at
confession became a hallmark of pastoral practice, as the church
sought to implement reforms that strengthened aspects of the
tradition that had been rejected or criticized by the Reformers.
Thus, in the two centuries before the Second Vatican Council,
frequency of attendance at the sacrament of confession became
a measure of one's identity with the church.

The reforms of Vatican II

The sacramental renewal that the council inaugurated has
been particularly significant with regard to this sacrament.
Modern scholarship had awakened a sense of the practice of
the early church and, as ever, Vatican II wanted a renewed emphasis on the significance of the word and the community in
the sacramental celebration. The popular name of the sacrament—confession—also came under scrutiny because it
seemed to highlight only one aspect of the rite. These varied

concerns led to important reforms. There would be a renewed emphasis on the word of God, conversion, and the community. The words "penance" and "reconciliation" would replace "confession" as better descriptions of the full meaning of the sacrament. And three forms for its celebration were introduced. We will analyze some of these issues in more detail.

The word of God

Given that the God of the Scriptures is revealed as forgiving and merciful, it is important to incorporate the proclamation of God's word into every celebration of this sacrament. No matter what the context the minister, always a priest or a bishop, should read from the Scriptures or quote them from memory or refer to a well-known passage concerning forgiveness. This sets the context for what priest and penitent are going to say to each other. The sacrament is not a scrupulous analysis of human imperfections or a heightened form of self-criticism or an effort to overcome the debilitating aspects of one's personality, but rather it is an encounter with the forgiving love of God as revealed in Jesus Christ. The minister bears an onerous responsibility in this regard. Through his words and actions he must reveal something of the merciful love of God that through the ministry of Christ has begun to transform the world. The more the minister and penitent reflect on God's word the better will they appreciate the depth of human sinfulness and the breadth of divine love.

Conversion

The celebration of the sacrament should lead to an ever deeper understanding of the need for conversion in the lives of all Christians. The sacrament can easily fail to do this. People have often rattled off a list of rather basic human failings or even, in some cases, confessed sins that they never committed. Presumably the reason for this is that people don't know what to say and so turn to some ready formula or project some fault upon themselves that doesn't really exist. This clearly demonstrates the need for catechesis with regard to the meaning of conversion in the sacrament of reconciliation. Participants should be encouraged to reflect upon their lives in a very personal manner. They might ask: What's really worrying me? What keeps me going from day to day? Does my Christian faith seriously impinge on my life? How do I treat my family and friends? Do I ever think about those who suffer? The questions could go on but they are intended to lead the individual to speak honestly and in some depth about his or her life. Christian faith is not just a moral code against which we judge ourselves; it is a lifelong journey that invites us to discover ever new horizons of what it means to be human. On this journey there is no point of arrival, only the invitation to move ahead or the danger of slipping backward. But one thing is for sure—rhyming off the same list of human failings over and over again is unlikely to lead one much further down the road of conversion. Similarly, the failure ever to speak honestly about one's Christian calling is unlikely to facilitate much growth and maturing.

The community

Traditionally this sacrament was understood in terms of privacy and secrecy. While protecting the confidentiality implicit in the rite, the reforms of Vatican II intend to foster an awareness of the communal dimensions of reconciliation. Sin, though often deeply personal, is not private because its effects can reach far and wide. As sinners we need to become aware of the damage that our words, actions, and omissions can do to others. This is one of the reasons why the sacrament exists. Our failures to live in accord with what we believe actually undermine the church as the body of Christ in the world. In the early church, as we have seen, this caused real difficulties and led the church to formulate a distinct rite for reconciling those who had been baptized but who lapsed into serious sin. The very origins of the sacrament lie in the need for the baptized individual to take his or her responsibilities seriously. That is why the church demands that we confess serious sin—because the hurt that was done is not just a private matter between the sinner and God but has implications for the life of the Christian community. Because we live such private lives in today's western societies, this emphasis sounds strange. But retrieving the sacraments from the clutches of an all too private type of piety is an important pastoral goal.

The three forms of celebration

The present rite of penance and reconciliation allows for three different types of celebration. These are the rites for an individual penitent, a communal rite with individual confession and absolution, and the communal rite with general confession and absolution. The first of these is the traditional way of celebrating the sacrament and understood by the church to be the normal form of participation. This way of celebrating the sacrament can veer between the mechanistic, when priest and people seem to only go through the motions, and the truly meaningful, when the penitent and minister truly reflect on the nature of life's journey. Given that the sacrament can be so beneficial in the life of the individual Christian, priests should take care to foster a sense of worship and reflection. This can be done in many ways.

The word of God should never be neglected. In chapter two we saw that the word can bring healing. Every celebration of the sacrament should begin with words from Scripture. They prepare both penitent and minister to open their hearts to God's mercy. By his general demeanor the priest should encourage penitents to feel at ease and to express their concerns in their own words rather than in traditional formulae. He should take care in giving penance; through creative suggestions about reading, writing, walking, talking, he might open the path to further self-reflection. Why not invite the penitent to read a chapter from the Bible or another book that is particularly relevant to his or her circumstances or to write a note to someone significant or to go for a walk in the countryside or to talk to someone who has been neglected?

It must be accepted that people will vary in how frequently they celebrate this sacrament. For some it has become a type of devotion in which they participate regularly. It will naturally prove difficult for the priest and penitent to foster a more reflective atmosphere in this context. Most Catholics, however, seem to have quietly abandoned, or seldom frequent, this rite. People feel alienated from the sacrament for various reasons: some were forced as children or adolescents to participate in it so regularly that it became meaningless; others had bad experiences with priests who were more akin to law officers than ministers of the new covenant; still others see the confessional as a symbol of darkness and fear that has little to do with their faith; many simply cannot see the point in the whole exercise.

To reach out to these members of the community it should be made clear that they are only expected to participate in the sacrament once a year. They should be encouraged to do so during the lenten and Easter seasons. Similarly people should know that they can celebrate the sacrament outside the atmosphere of the confessional and that they should feel free to approach any priest. But, most important of all, Christians should be invited to think seriously about their lives and to express their thoughts about themselves within the confines of the sacrament. In an era of explosive growth in all forms of psychotherapy we need to rediscover the spiritual therapy of the sacrament of reconciliation. Bound as the minister is by the seal of the sacrament, it remains one of the truly confidential contexts for self-disclosure and analysis.

The communal rite with individual confession and absolution has become common in many parishes. Its great strength is that it involves the broader community in the celebration of the sacrament. It also provides the opportunity for a more wholesome reflection on the word of God and a searching examination of conscience. Many pastors see a problem with this rite in that the confession of sin is understandably abbreviated as all penitents are asked to wait until individual confessions are complete so that the ritual can be closed in a communal fashion in keeping with the spirit of the gathering. But is this really a problem? Catholics are bound to confess mortal sins; lesser failings do not have to be confessed in the sacrament, not least because they are acknowledged and forgiven at the beginning of every Mass. Nothing has changed our perception of the sacrament of reconciliation more than developments in moral theology. Until Vatican II it was presumed that mortal sin was common; today we would be slow to suggest that any particular individual has committed such a sin. Therefore it is surely the case that large numbers of penitents attending the sacrament are not guilty of mortal sin and so there is no reason for them to go through a list of less serious faults. It is a good practice during these communal rites to suggest to any penitent confessing very serious sin that he or she might return to talk further with a priest at a later, quieter time.

The third form of celebration of the sacrament is a communal rite with general confession and absolution. Those who receive such absolution must confess any serious sins to a priest as soon as possible. This rite can only be provided in cases of grave necessity. As always, such grave necessity includes danger of death. The other most obvious example is where a shortage of clergy would preclude people from celebrating the sacrament and therefore might also exclude them from the Eucharist. The Vatican has made clear that such necessity is not created by there being simply a large gathering of people, such as at a pilgrimage center or in a parish on Christmas Day or Easter Sunday. The determination of what exactly "grave necessity" means has naturally led to variations in the provision of this form of the rite. It is the responsibility of the diocesan bishop to determine if such necessity exists in a particular place and time. Therefore the practice can vary from one diocese to another.

Conclusion

The numbers attending the sacrament of reconciliation regularly are in steep decline in many parts of the world. This should not lead to undue pastoral anxiety. When one takes a longer view of things, one sees that numbers attending various sacraments have fluctuated greatly throughout history. Maybe today we should change our pastoral goal so that our energies are devoted to celebrating the sacrament with significant numbers of people once a year rather than trying to coax some people to participate in the sacrament more regularly.

Finally, there remains the controversial issue of at what age baptized persons should be admitted to the sacrament. Currently the practice is to celebrate "first confession" at seven years of age. The reason for this is that seven was the age of discretion in Roman law, and once a baptized person reached this age, he or she was held to be in some way responsible. Modern theories drawn from the social and human sciences question whether a child of seven is indeed truly responsible, but it takes a long time for such theories to affect the traditions of the church. It looks likely that we will continue with the present age of entry to the sacrament for some time to come. Be that as it may, the more important task remains of calling all Christians to ever deeper conversion.

Chapter Four

Celebrating Death

It is impossible to remember our months in the womb; in fact it is difficult to recall our first couple of years. Our only access to those years is through the stories our parents tell us or through photographs. That life we once lived, though intrinsically part of who we are, bears little resemblance to the life that we now live. Physically, emotionally, and intellectually we differ greatly from ourselves as infants. In effect, the infant I once was has been transformed just as surely as the vigorous youth will one day change into an old man or woman. The journey from the womb to the tomb is a process of dying and letting go. It is a journey of learning and maturing into new experience and identity. In modern life the changes happen so slowly to us that they go unnoticed, and so familiarity with our lives blunts the transformations that gradually do occur.

In contrast, those in primitive societies experienced rites of passage as they encountered the key stages of life, and so had a sense of passing from one state to another, of dying to an old identity and giving birth to a new one. The most important passage was from childhood to adulthood, and these rites initiated a person into the values and myths of a society and its spiritual realm. In order to learn how to come into the fullness of being, emotionally, socially, and psychologically, a person first had to learn how to die. One could not become an adult unless the child first died. In initiation ceremonies, then, symbols of death saturated the neophyte's environment, and they were filthy with the earth into which everything is rendered down. One can quite rightly say, then, that those in archaic societies first learned how to die through their rituals of initiation.

In Christianity the reality is no different. In baptism we are reborn into Christ, and the church claims us as Christ's own with the sign of the cross. From the first few moments of Christian life we are marked by death. Those of us who are buried with Christ in the death of baptism are also reborn into everlasting life. And so it is in baptism that we first learn how to die. As St. Paul puts it: "When we were baptized in Christ Jesus we were baptized in his death; in other words, when we were baptized we went into the tomb with him and joined him in death, so that as Christ was raised from the dead by the Father's glory, we too might live a new life" (Rom 6:3–4). In the sacrament of confirmation we are reminded that we must be witnesses to Christ's suffering, death, and resurrection, and in the Eucharist we are constantly called to participate in the death and self-sacrifice of Christ so as to share the new life that he brings.

Nobody can speak of what things will be like after we die except that we are baptized into an everlasting life with Christ, and so the new identity that we were reborn into will have an eternal existence. However, there is a finality about death and an everlasting dying of the historical project that is one's life. The church teaches quite definitively that we are completely responsible for what we have done during our life span. What good we have done remains done, yet what we have broken remains broken, and unjust actions cannot be revisited.

Despite the fact that we cannot know what things will be like after death, it is only natural to want to imagine what sort of perspectives and experiences we might have. It is true that what lies beyond the threshold of eternity remains a mystery, but dying does not, because the passages that we make in life require a type of dying. In adulthood the child must die, in marriage the single person must die, in old age the youth must die. In forgiveness, bitterness perishes, and in self-sacrifice, selfishness is overcome. We know these places and have tasted the difficulty and darkness of letting go to maturity and altruism. The dying that we do throughout life is always a dying-for-another. If I mature or marry I do so for another. If I forgive, I do so for another, and if I let go of individualism, I do so for another. In all of this there is a basic trust that this dying will bring good, that the transformation that will occur in this relationship will be fruitful and lead to intimacy. And this is true of life. Reconciliation and healing are wonderful realities but they are etched on the headstone of hatred and bitterness. Selflessness and self-sacrifice transform relationships and clothe us in the warmth of love, but first the ego must perish as it is stripped of what were once understood to be needful things. Life looked at in this manner does not teach us what lies beyond the threshold of death, but it does tell us that the lifelong human process of dying brings the gift of maturity and more loving and genuine relationships. When we die for another we do so in trust, and when we die in Christ we do so in the trust that we will live in him: "If anyone believes in me, even though he dies he will live, and whoever lives and believes in me will never die" (Jn 11:25–26).

A ritual dying

Since our primitive forebears first observed the waxing and waning of the moon and the corresponding cycles of death and resurrection through the passages of a person's life, one truth has remained constant: death precedes new life and dying ushers in transformation. This is what the ritual process tells us about dying. Those in archaic societies knew this truth well, and so they didn't fear death as much as modern man and woman do because they had learned through their rites of passage that life and death are inseparable. This sense of death as transformation was born and nourished through their rites of initiation, their rituals of dying and new life. Long after their rites of initiation were complete, primitives returned to their symbols of death and rebirth to experience the deeper dimensions of human existence and religious experience. Many today bemoan the disintegration of values and meaning that comes with modern life, and so it is beneficial to look to those untouched by contemporary culture to learn what we have forgotten. Their closeness to, and reverence for, the symbols of death highlight our need to experience constantly the power of the Christian symbols of death and resurrection. We have become anesthetized to the cross and the empty tomb through a familiarity that blunts the scandalous and wondrous reality of Easter. The Christian community should therefore spare no effort to re-imagine through song, story, and dance the healing and redemptive symbols of Easter. We will only learn how to die as Christians by celebrating the ritual of death and new life that is the paschal mystery.

A paschal dying

Story has it that when Pope John XXIII was dying he said, "My bags are packed, and I am waiting for her." There is a sense in his words of fulfillment and promise. His words seem full of expectation and anticipation. His sentiments seem to contrast the wake room and graveside scenes that many of us witness with anger and incomprehensibility. In the latter, death can be perceived as that which makes all of living and loving absurd. Why invest so much energy and intimacy in life when it can be wrenched away so easily, so futilely, or with no word of warning? If death can make nonsense out of the historical project of life and love, then one could easily lose respect for the gift of living. If life is an absurdity, then it can be lived irresponsibly, dangerously, and without regard. It can be perceived as a venture bereft of meaning, lacking in value and worth. In order to search for meaning we would do well to revisit the symbols of Easter, of death and resurrection.

In the incarnation God and humanity become one in the person of Jesus Christ. In Jesus, God lived a human life and lived it fully and died a human death and died it completely. Jesus died; he did not slumber in the tomb for a short while. For some his dying was seen as a disgrace and a scandal. It was an absurdity, denying the conventional wisdom of what a Messiah should be. His followers subsequently cowered in a room entertaining doubt and denial. We were spared such embarrassment, born as we were into a believing community, and even now the familiarity of the crucifix has numbed us to the scandal that is our God bloodied and beaten like a lamb led to the slaughter. On Calvary God experienced the darkest aspects of being human and the utter absurdity of life. What can be more inexplicable and meaningless than the innocent butchery of the Son of God? And yet the cross has been transformed by Easter to become the symbol of our freedom and redemption. Christ's sacrifice on the altar of Calvary cancelled the effect of sin and made us one with God. It was the moment of our atonement but it was also the moment when Christ made sense of the absurdity of death. His dying was an act of love through which he gave his life for others. It was dying-for-another, and his death identified the nature of his personal historical project. Jesus came to save us from sin and death, and he did so by offering his own life. The historical project of his life was accomplished at the moment of his death. Calvary now defines Christ as our redeemer and savior, and so it no longer scandalizes or confuses. Having reached into the murkiest and most lonesome parts of human existence, and even into death itself, Christ has transformed dying into that which gives meaning to one's entire life: "What shall I say? Father, save me from this hour? But it was for this very reason that I have come to this hour" (Jn 12:27).

The paschal symbols give us a new perspective on living and dying. It is as if with Easter we put on new spectacles and see the world anew. We live our lives and commit ourselves to relationships under the shadow of death. In this way, death actually defines the nature of how we live and how we relate to others. We live and love in the knowledge that one day it will all be gone. We live, create, imagine, and love despite the eventual annihilation of this project, and yet our lives are more worthy and selfless because of this. Dying becomes the ultimate self-sacrifice as we must leave the life into which we have invested so much. All our living then can be seen as paschal, and the fulfillment and consummation of this life is in dying.

An Easter people

We emphasized in chapter one that the most meaningful realities in life—grace, healing, forgiveness, and genuine relationships—are experienced through brokenness, hurt, sickness, and loss. There is a very definite dynamic here of dying and new life. The early Christian communities initially expected Christ to return and raise the dead within the course of their lives. Gradually, however, they came to understand that Christ was still truly present to them in the breaking of the bread and that his death and resurrection were realities to be experienced on this side of the grave. The reality of Christ's resurrection could be witnessed as these people, full of fear and doubt, were transformed into a Pentecostal community characterized by faith and celebration.

There is a temptation to wait for everything to be put right after death, to play a waiting game according to some promise that all injustice and disappointment will somehow be erased at the moment of dying. Yet, in effect, this is to avoid the responsibility that we are called to make salvation a reality now. Those who are alienated, impoverished, and marginalized need salvation now while they are alive. Life and living have been redeemed by Calvary, and so our experience of being saved is not dependent upon dying. Persons will know they are saved when they are taken from impoverishment or exclusion, loneliness or hurt. We were called in baptism into the death and resurrection of Jesus Christ, and it is only by dying with him that we will live with him. But that dying starts today. In the Eucharist we are called to self-sacrifice, to continuously die to selfishness so as to live for others, to know the needs of those gathered around the table that is the altar of Christ's death. Like those early Christian communities we must learn that resurrection happens in the authenticity of caring for others and attending to another person. Like Christ, our lives will be accomplished when we die for others and, like Christ, we will rise to new life from the tomb of self-emptying love: "If we have died with him, then we shall live with him. If we hold firm, then we shall reign with him" (2 Tim 2:11–12). We cannot and do not know the details of eternity, just as surely as we cannot and do not understand what happens at the moment of death. We stand, as it were, on the border crossing between the lands of life and death, yet we must turn back into the land of the living for it is here that we must learn how to die.

Funeral rites

Cultures vary enormously in their manner of disposing of the dead. Even within Christianity one will find significantly different patterns of behavior between one ethnic group and another. This is to be welcomed, as no traditions are more expressive of a group's indigenous practices than funeral customs. The rites of the church allow for such cultural adaptation, and pastors should foster an intermingling of Christian and native traditions. However, the greater difficulty that we must face today is a new one posed by modern Western societies.

There is a real denial of death in advanced western societies. In fact, the sense of denial is so great that it is one of the factors that would lead one to question how advanced this civilization really is. With the onslaught of massive conurbations all sense of kindred ties and community begin to unravel. The results are there for all to see. While we live much more efficient lives compared to our forebears, allowing for extraordinary mobility, the danger is that our only measure of anything is in terms of its consumer value. In such societies, death gets pushed out into the realm of one more consumer item. We live in an era of professionalism based on the division of labor. There are experts in every field, and we turn to them as our needs require. This has happened with regard to death as well. It is taken over by the "professionals" in the funeral industry, and the corpse is treated as something from which people almost need to be protected.

In this context, the Christian community should adopt a radical countercultural approach by embracing death as an integral part of human life. There are different ways in which this can be done, depending, of course, on the particular culture. Death pushes people to the outer edges of their experience. This is a place where common sense and ordinary language begin to falter. The rituals of the church are all important in beginning the process of grieving, so priests and other ministers should take care to adapt the rites to the needs of the particular occasion. Hospital mortuaries and funeral homes, comfortable as they might be, are not the ideal setting for the gathering of a mournful Christian community; family homes and churches are just such settings. Families could be encouraged to bring the corpse of the deceased home. Nothing is more important in bereavement than coming to terms with the fact that the person has actually died. Also the family is truly serving the broader community by awakening everyone to the fact that death is at the heart of life. Significant numbers of people have never been present at an actual death and many have never seen or touched a corpse. These experiences, painfully difficult as they are, contribute to the formation of our true identity.

There are important issues raised in the funeral rites of children who die before baptism. Death that occurs so early in life is torturous for parents to bear. Ritual is very significant at this time because our ordinary patterns of behavior crumble in the face of such suffering. Before the baby is buried, if at all possible, the parents should participate in a ritual that includes the naming of their child. At the very least, this should be done at a later gathering of family and friends. It is very unfortunate if a child is not retrieved from the darkness of anonymity. Babies who are stillborn or who die shortly after birth are human persons who, for whatever mysterious reasons, will never travel with us to the outer edges of human experience but whose death pushes us, against our wills, to those further thresholds. That is why we sometimes speak of them as angels, messengers who tell us something of who God is and what life is ultimately about. Such is the mystery of death and dying.

PART III

The Sacraments of Vocation

Traditionally we used the term "vocation" to refer to the call received by those who enter priestly or religious life—those who are ordained or live under religious vows. More recently the term has also been used with regard to Christian marriage. Ever since the calling of the first disciples on the shores of the sea of Galilee, the church has believed that its members are called to the service of the gospel in different ways. Some are called to be priests, others to live their lives under vows of chastity, poverty, and obedience, while the majority put their lives at the service of God through the commitment and dedication demanded by married life. Traditionally a vocation was understood in a very simple way as if one could literally hear the voice of God. Today we place much more emphasis on the mediation of God's word to us through family and friends, prayer and personal reflection, the example and direction of others who have struggled with a particular vocation, and not least through our involvement in the Christian community and the effort to live in accord with the gospel. Through these varied realities, each individual Christian must seek to construct his or her own response to the gift of life and the gospel call to put one's life at the service of others.

There are three clear vocations in the Catholic church—to married, priestly, and religious life. Notice that they have much in common. All three demand that one's energy and efforts be put at the service of others; they involve the making of a promise in the presence of others, as the Christian community celebrates and affirms publicly the vocation that the particular individual embraces; they require a commitment for life; they produce a completely changed reality in the lives of those involved, as after the marriage or ordination or profession ceremony the person is recognized as having a radically different identity in the Christian community. Nothing leads to a greater misunderstanding of the meaning of Christian vocation than mistaking it for a job or type of employment. One often hears people saying that certain forms of employment—especially in healthcare or education provision—are really vocations. Insofar as this means that such positions demand great skills and dedication on the part of those involved it is clearly true, but this has nothing to do with the Christian idea of vocation. With regard to one's job, and this is true of all forms of employment, one earns a wage and has certain rights and obligations. One has the right to a fair wage, to decent working conditions, to holidays and free time and, if these are denied, a right to strike. One's obligations are dictated by contractual arrangements with employers. None of this is true of a Christian vocation, since it is not a job but a way of life. It is not based on contractual obligations but on personal commit-

ment. It does not lead to a fair wage for work done but to the
endless demand to give of oneself. It does not end at 5:00 PM
on a Friday evening but is ever present. And one does not have
the right to strike. A Christian vocation then is not a job or a
form of employment. It is the manner in which a particular individual is called within the Christian community to live out
his or her response to God's call.

When we speak of marriage as a vocation we do not mean
that an individual was predestined to marry his or her spouse
but that the relationship between God and the particular individual is inseparable from the reality of married life. The relationship with God matures or declines in the context of the
particular commitment that the person has made to live in the
married state. In other words, the most important realities in
life through which we encounter the face of God—love and
friendship, joy and heartbreak, maturing and aging, sickness
and death, sin and failure—are intimately intertwined with the
experience of marriage. Similarly with those who are ordained
or live under religious vows—they must work out their response to God's invitation in the particular context of their vocation.

Notice that these three vocations include the vast majority
of adult members of the Catholic church. But one notable
group is missing—those who are single (unmarried) and are
not ordained or members of religious orders. It is arguable that
this is the most neglected group of people in the history of the
church. They receive little of the ecclesial and other supports
and recognition that are attached to being married, ordained,
or living in a religious community. The problem is, of course,
that many single people will end up entering one of the three
recognized vocations. And this has always been the problem—
is a single life in itself truly a vocation? The answer is surely
"no." Can it be a vocation? The answer is almost certainly
"yes." For it to be so, however, certain conditions, akin to

those linked to the other vocations, would have to be met. It would need to be a long-term commitment entered into freely; the individual would have to be willing to put some of the energy and time that come from being single at the service of others, while the Christian community, for its part, would have to celebrate and support this form of vocation. In other words, for a single life to be a vocation it could not be just something that one slips into unplanned or unexpectedly; rather at a certain point in life one would have to make a definitive choice to live one's response to God in this way. Clearly, for this to happen the church will need to put in place some ritual that recognizes and celebrates such a commitment. This may happen in the future. A beginning might be noted in the *Catechism of the Catholic Church* (paragraph 1658), which at least accepts the particular issues raised in the lives of single persons. This might sow the seeds of further reflection on the nature of single life as a possible form of Christian vocation.

In the two chapters that constitute part three of this book, we devote our attention to marriage and holy orders. Single life is not treated here because the church has not recognized it formally as a vocation, nor do we deal with religious profession, because, for various reasons that go beyond the scope of this book, it is not a sacrament in the Catholic church.

Chapter Five

Marriage

Is marriage a sacrament? The simple answer is "yes." But this deceptively simple answer raises a whole lot of other questions. Is marriage always a sacrament? The answer is "no." There are many examples—civil weddings, marriages between nonbaptized spouses, marriages where one or both partners cannot celebrate the sacrament because of age or previous commitments or some other impediment. Was marriage always a sacrament? The answer is "no"; it is only because of the life, death, and resurrection of Christ that the natural union of man and woman has been transformed and raised to a higher plane. And the questions go on and on: What makes marriage a sacrament? Who can get married? Why are some marriages declared null? Even from this cursory analysis, one can begin to sense how complicated this whole issue can become. Indeed, it is so complex that some noted Christian thinkers have suggested that the church should withdraw from the area completely and leave it to the civil sphere of life. As attractive as this might sound, it is not a serious option. How could the church abandon what is the most important reality in the lives of the vast majority of its members? The task today is to restate the theology of marriage in a way that is true to Christian tradition and yet takes account of the "signs of the times." This chapter is an attempt to do just that.

Marriage in the Scriptures
From the earliest texts of the Bible, marriage is endowed with a special status. That God made them male and female means

that this distinction at the very heart of creation is divinely
willed. As man and woman joined together in wedlock, so too
Yahweh entered into a covenant with the people, but this was
a relationship characterized by the people's ingratitude and infidelity. And so the prophets, in speaking of Yahweh, use the
image of the lover who incessantly follows the unfaithful
beloved through wilderness and desert, mountain and plain,
enslavement and captivity, until the beloved would rediscover
her true identity.

The covenant was the relationship that bound God and the
people together. The early Christians began to speak of the
new covenant that emerged from the death and resurrection of
Christ. Christ poured out his blood on the cross, and through
this act of self-sacrifice he brought new life and hope to the
world. Because of their faith in the resurrection, the first believers saw God as accepting Jesus' self-offering, and they looked
forward to his return in glory. In the meantime they had to face
all sorts of interesting questions, not the least significant of
which was: What does marriage mean in the light of our faith
in the death and resurrection of Christ? In order to understand
their perception of marriage, it is important to bear in mind a
couple of things.

Marriage existed for centuries before Christianity, so there
was nothing new about it, and the first believers thought that
Christ's return was imminent. What really mattered was the
latter, not the former. It was important to ready oneself for the
Lord's return, and so many believers abandoned all worldly
concerns in the anticipation of an apocalyptic end to all material things. For some, this included marriage. Thus in some of
the writings of St. Paul marriage is looked upon as very definitely in second place behind a life of personal commitment to
the Lord. Concerns about spouse and family do not compare
with the task of proclaiming the good news. Down through
history this line of thinking has dominated in the church's

leadership, which has generally perceived marriage as an inferior form of discipleship as compared to freely chosen virginity and celibacy. But early on, another strand of thought began to develop. As the first generation of believers themselves began to die, belief in the imminent return of the Lord declined. Christian communities were faced with how to cope with the world in the medium to longer term. It was during this period, toward the end of the first century and in the succeeding century, that the church put in place its structures of leadership and a new theology of marriage.

It is in a couple of short verses in the letter to the Ephesians that we find an extraordinary claim about the meaning of marriage for Christians. Having quoted the famous verse from the book of Genesis—"for this reason, a man must leave his father and mother and be joined to his wife, and the two will become one body"—the author goes on to say: "this mystery has many implications; but I am saying that it applies to Christ and the church" (see Eph 5:31–32). The word "mystery" is very significant in the Pauline corpus of writings. It refers to the whole mystery of what God reveals in Christ. In this passage marriage forms an integral part of that mystery. Far from being an insidious reality or a lesser form of discipleship, marriage is understood to be part of the relationship of Christ to his church. Christ's self-giving is prefigured and mirrored in the self-sacrifice that marriage entails. Notice too that the text refers to marriage going right back to the beginning. In other words, even before the coming of Christ marriage was already a symbol of the relationship of God to humanity. Given the times in which the text was written, this is indeed a notable claim. It is generally accepted that the letter to the Ephesians was composed toward the end of the first century, quite some time after the death of Paul. At that time and throughout the next century, Christians were tempted to interpret their new faith through the lenses of various philosophies that were dominant in the world around them. The twin philosophies of Manichaeism and dualism were hostile to anything material, including the human body and sexual intercourse. But the Pauline community from which this letter emerged rejected the idea that marriage and the human body were evil and that one would have to turn one's back on them in order to gain true spiritual enlightenment. Yet throughout the succeeding centuries, the debate over the Christian significance of marriage continued, since monasticism and celibacy dominated the popular mind as the only true path of discipleship.

Vatican II

In the *Constitution on the Church in the Modern World* (*Gaudium et Spes*, paragraphs 47-52) we find the most comprehensive statement that any church council ever made about marriage. Notably the idea of covenant is emphasized. Since medieval times, the dominant theology of marriage had centered on contract and on the obligations, particularly concerning childbearing, that this placed on the spouses. But Vatican II sounded a return to an older theology, that marriage was based more on relationship than contract. This brings one back inevitably to reflection upon the covenant and the theology of the letter to the Ephesians. When one thinks of marriage as a covenant, one cannot but compare and contrast it with the relationship of God to the people. Only one word can describe the nature of the God of the old and new covenants—"faithful," particularly in the midst of the faithlessness of the people. This is the God of love who, like a true lover, will ceaselessly seek out the beloved. Similarly, those who enter the covenant relationship of marriage will be asked to remain faithful even in the midst of great difficulties. Like the people of God of old, they have to go on a journey that will reveal all their weaknesses and failings, and yet, even in the midst of these, they will be asked to remain faithful, to trust in the God of the covenant when all else fails. This is the great story of human and divine love that ebbs and flows through human history. Undoubtedly Vatican II was right to contextualize marriage in this story, but the council also reaffirmed traditional teaching concerning commitment and indissolubility. It made clear that marriage between Christians is indeed a sacrament.

What makes marriage a sacrament?
Marriage is unique among the seven sacraments. In the other six, the ordinary minister is a bishop, priest, or deacon (i.e., someone who is ordained), but in the case of marriage it is the man and woman who are getting married. The proof that we have failed to communicate this reality is obvious from the language that we use. We speak of the priest as having married a certain couple when this is not the case. The priest does not marry any couple; rather the man and woman marry each other. The task of the priest (or bishop or deacon) is to assist at the ceremony and bless the marriage. But with the complete domination of clergy in the church in recent centuries one could be forgiven for thinking that the key figure at many weddings is indeed the priest.

What do we mean by saying that the man and woman who are marrying each other are the ministers of the sacrament? It means that they confer the sacrament on each other through the mutual giving of consent. Without this consent there is no marriage. The role of the priest and the broader Christian community is secondary. What really matters is the consent of a man and woman to enter into a covenantal relationship with one another. To understand the significance of this, it is interesting to draw contrasts with other Christian churches. In the Eastern Orthodox churches, the minister of marriage is the priest who, through crowning the man and woman, marries them. In most Protestant churches there is a similar emphasis on the role of the cleric. But in the theology of the Catholic church the consent of the couple constitutes the sacrament. That is why in the Catholic rite the man and woman are not declared to be husband and wife; nobody and no power can make a marriage except the consent of the couple. There are many implications that follow from this. One must remember, in reading these, that we are talking about marriages involving baptized Christians.

a) Without true consent there is no marriage, notwith-standing all appearances to the contrary. The two families can gather, the words can be spoken, the celebrations can be en-joyed, but no marriage takes place unless consent is freely given.

b) As ministers of the sacrament, the couple must intend to do that which the church intends in the sacrament, that is, they must intend to marry each other. Clearly on the day of the wedding nobody can appreciate the full personal, social, and financial implications of marriage, but the couple must in-tend to enter a lifelong relationship with one another.

c) If one cannot give consent, then one cannot be married in the Catholic church. Quite a number of people cannot give the necessary consent. The obvious impediments to consent are age (one or other of the parties is too young), pressure to enter the marriage (which might be psychological, social, or financial), or some medical conditions that mean a particular individual can never take on real responsibilities. There are other impediments defined in the church's law, the most con-troversial of which are an existing marriage bond, religious profession, or ordination.

d) Since it is the case that consent might not have been given (though the words were spoken), or that one of the par-ties was incapable of giving consent (though the words were spoken), then the church has to have a system in place whereby some marriages are declared invalid. This is usually called "annulment." The process through which a marriage is declared null will always be controversial because it almost inevitably involves judgments about the emotional maturity of those involved.

e) Nobody can give another person permission to marry. The individual must decide. We used to speak a lot about "letters of freedom," which priests were asked to give parishioners before marriage. Such letters did not bestow the freedom to get married; rather they were statements that, as far as the priest knew, this particular person was free to marry. The task of the priest is to establish, as best he can, that those who wish to get married are free to do so. If they are not, then he cannot give them such freedom.

f) Because marriage is based on consent it is indissoluble. When two Christians freely promise to enter a relationship, their committed love is no longer just a private matter between them but it becomes part of the story of God's relationship with humanity. As the God of the covenants was faithful beyond what reason would demand, so too the marriage bond is raised to a new level. Authentic married love is caught up in divine love. This is what is meant by saying that marriage is a sacrament. The man and woman speak simple words, but the reality that they enter is far greater than themselves.

These implications raise as many questions as they answer. But maybe the most important one of all is this: Can consent be withdrawn? Clearly at a human level it often is. The bizarre level of marital breakdown and remarriage in many Western countries demonstrates that large numbers of Christians believe that they can freely leave one marriage and enter another. And, of course, in civil law this is absolutely true. But this matter has little to do with civil law. It is a question of one's understanding of the relationship of God with humanity, of how one is going to live out one's discipleship of Christ as a vocation within the church. One can only understand the strict approach that the Catholic church takes on the issue of dissolving marriages when one appreciates the theology of consent that we have been analyzing here. Other churches take a more lenient view of things, but it is notable that their theology of marriage does not place the same emphasis on consent.

The necessity of faith

All sacraments demand and nourish faith. Without it they are meaningless. But, as ever, there is great difficulty in determining what faith is required and whether it exists or not. As a result, some pastors use a very strict criterion for admission to the sacraments, including marriage: one will only be admitted if one practices the faith frequently in the particular parish.

With regard to the sacrament of marriage, a few simple points should be made. The faith required is essentially expressed through the giving of consent to one's partner rather than through weekly attendance at Sunday Mass. This amounts to a very significant act of faith in another person. If a baptized person is free to give such consent and desires to do so, then, even if he or she does not practice the faith regularly, it is difficult to justify the refusal of some pastors to allow the ceremony to go ahead in their parish churches. It does, however, make a lot of sense to celebrate such a marriage outside of Mass. The normal context for a marriage between Catholics is the Eucharist, but this need not be the case. When Catholics who have long since lapsed from participation at Mass ask to get married in the church, then such marriages might not include a celebration of the Eucharist. The reason for this is clear. The faith required for meaningful participation in the Eucharist is of a different order from that necessitated by marriage. In the latter, one is asked to believe in the value of a human relationship based on trust and fidelity; in the former one is invited to believe that Christ is really present and to partake in the very life of God.

In order to nurture the faith of those preparing for marriage, parishes and dioceses should provide relevant preparation. This should emphasize the importance of consent. It should raise significant questions in the minds of those intending to get married. Am I too young to make such a commitment? Are my partner and I mature enough to set out on this path? Have I revealed my true self to the one I intend to wed? The participants might be encouraged to reflect upon the actual formula of consent. "I take you as my husband/wife, for better or for worse, for richer or for poorer, in sickness and in health, all the days of my life." Marriage is often for the better, for richer, and experienced in good health. But at times it is for worse, it can lead to impoverishment, and it will have to endure sickness. Those who intend to set out on this journey should have some sense that their commitment will be tested by life.

Most important of all, the actual ritual of marriage should be celebrated in such a way that its meaning and demands are clear, while giving true affirmation to the couple as they set out on the unknown journey.

The celebration of marriage

As marriage is the most important threshold that most believers will ever cross, it is surprising that the ritual is so simple. Leaving aside the celebration of the Eucharist that accompanies many weddings, the actual rite of marriage is very short. Here it is in outline:

    i) Liturgy of the word
    ii) Liturgy of marriage
        address and examination
        consent of the couple
        blessing of rings, gold, silver, etc.
        prayer of the newly married couple
        general intercessions

iii) Nuptial blessing

This is the ritual celebration of marriage in the Catholic church. Even within this simple ritual two things are much more important than the others—the address and examination and the giving of consent. The assistant (usually a priest or deacon or bishop, though it can be a delegated layperson) asks the man and woman if they have come freely and without pressure to get married. Then the couple gives consent. It is these two steps that constitute the sacrament of marriage. Everything else is secondary and should underpin the meaning of the giving of consent. Here are some pointers that might help:

1) The rite allows for all sorts of regional variations in different parts of the world provided consent is asked for and given. Similarly it should be made clear to all those preparing for marriage that they do not have to accept various traditions that are not central to the rite, such as the giving away of the bride and particular forms of dress.

2) Indigenous adaptations of the ritual could replace rings and money with more culturally nuanced symbols of wedlock.

3) The couple should be involved in the preparation of all aspects of the ritual. This could include the composing of a prayer for the newly married.

4) Because the words of consent are crucial they should be clearly heard. Couples should be encouraged to use the statement form of consent (where they say all of the words) rather than the interrogative form (where the priest says most of the words). After the words of consent have been spoken is a good time to play some reflective music so as to give all present a moment to savor the promises that have just been made.

5) As at any sacramental gathering, the organization of the available space is important. Given that the attendance at weddings will not normally fill the church building, steps should

be taken to gather the congregation around the sanctuary in a more intimate setting. Maximum audibility, visibility, and participation are required. It can be beneficial to get the couple to face the congregation during the ritual of marriage. They will naturally feel shy in doing so but it clearly marks out the significance of the giving of consent. Furthermore, it will give the participants a real feeling of being pushed out to the threshold.

6) Priests, or other assistants, should take care not to become the center of attention. It is arguable that concelebration should be avoided at weddings as it only detracts from the centrality of the bride and groom. At any rate only the presiding priest/deacon should go forward for the examination and the giving of consent. The homily should take account of the fact that there are often many people present who do not regularly attend church. The care and solicitude of the Christian community for all people should be made clear.

Conclusion

The Christian understanding of marriage was fraught with difficulties from the beginning since the idea and reality of betrothal and wedlock long predated the emergence of the new faith. Right down to today, problems persist not just with marriage but with a whole range of associated issues like premarital sex, extramarital affairs, divorce, gay/lesbian relationships, among many others. While these realities raise a whole range of moral questions and ethical challenges, it is important to keep in mind that the basic theological principle concerning the nature of human relationships is premised upon consent and commitment. Where true consent and honest commitment are present, a relationship is surely Christian; where these are lacking, human dignity is undermined and people are abused. Fostering a sense of the value of consent and commitment is, then, an important pastoral goal in the life of the church. Nothing could be more important in this regard than supporting those who are preparing to get married. Those who freely embark on the journey of married life today are making an extraordinary act of faith in their partner and in God. It is now completely countercultural to enter into marriage with the intention of remaining faithful for life. All of the cultural undertones in Western countries suggest otherwise—sex is free; nobody could be expected to have only one partner in life; consent can be withdrawn whenever the individual gets tired or bored. In such a context it is probably true to say that those who freely enter the married state with open hearts and minds and a desire to stand by their commitments through thick and thin, are among the most faithful of all God's people.

Chapter Six

Holy Orders

One of the major debates of the Reformation period centered on the nature of priesthood, whether indeed there should be priests at all. Today the idea of a church without priests, or at least without a set of people ordained and set apart for special ministry, seems almost absurd. Many Protestant churches speak easily of ordination, priesthood, ministry, and clergy; ordained ministers commonly dress in a manner that clearly distinguishes them from others who are baptized while much of the trenchant tone of the Reformation sounds like a distant echo. Does this mean that the Catholic church's understanding of priesthood is now accepted by all? Certainly not, but it does mean that the need to justify the very existence of the priesthood is no longer a burning issue; the question today is not whether there should be a priesthood but rather what sort of priesthood we should have. One would imagine that a good place to start analyzing this issue would be in contemporary theology. Unfortunately this is not the case. Our understanding of Christ, the church, and the sacraments has undergone profound renewal due to modern theological research. But the same cannot be said of priestly life; we have oceans of canon law but still very little theology based on a renewed reading of the Scriptures. Here we will highlight some themes that are pertinent in the development of a theology of the priesthood relevant to our times.

The three orders

There are three holy orders in the Catholic church; that is why
we speak of the sacrament of holy orders in the plural, since
one can be ordained three times to the three orders of the diaconate (normally called deacons), the presbyterate (normally
called priests), and the episcopate (normally called bishops).
Bishops and presbyters both share in the priesthood, whereas
deacons do not. Both bishops and presbyters are ordained
priests but according to Vatican II the fullness of the priesthood is found in the episcopate. This is an interesting statement, for it means that the ministry of the priest/presbyter orig-
inates and culminates in the priestly ministry of the bishop. A
clear change in emphasis from the Council of Trent was
sounded here; the anti-Protestant polemics of the sixteenth
century vested enormous power in the priest/presbyter, while
a bishop was really understood as merely a more senior priest
given special authority. That is why even today Catholics find
it difficult to understand that a chosen priest/presbyter is actually *ordained* as a bishop and so tend to use any verb except or-
dain, like consecrated, elevated, and even coronated, for surely one can be ordained only once? The answer is definitely
"no"; in fact, to become a bishop one must be ordained three
times—first as a deacon, then as presbyter, and then as a bishop. Becoming aware of the plurality of ministries already present in the three orders of the Catholic church might sow the
seeds of possible new horizons for ministries in the future.

Bishops

The Catholic church is structured on the basis of dioceses
overseen by bishops. The meaning of the word *episcopos*
(bishop) is "one who oversees." From the first century onward
there were such overseers in the various churches, and in time
their position became ever more important as the church
began to see in them the guarantee of apostolic fidelity. The

belief of the Catholic church is that the first apostles chose successors to whom they handed on their teaching and power (especially the invocation of the Holy Spirit through the laying on of hands and the forgiveness of sin) and that these have been handed down faithfully from one generation to the next from the first apostles to our own time almost two thousand years later. Thus we speak of the apostolic link between us and the first apostles. In the Catholic church this link is personified in the bishop, while in most Protestant churches the emphasis is placed on the scriptural word as the key to apostolic fidelity. In other words, most Protestants believe that the best way to follow the teaching of the apostles is to base one's life on the New Testament, whereas in the Catholic church huge significance has always been attached to how that teaching has been handed down and interpreted by the successors of the apostles—the bishops.

The bishop is the key figure in the local church. In the Catholic church these local or particular churches are called dioceses. It is a gross misunderstanding to perceive these dioceses or particular churches as branches or subsections of the universal church. Each diocese under a bishop is the one, holy, catholic, and apostolic church in a particular place. It does not constitute only a bit of or a part of the church. It is the church in all of its reality in this place. Through its communion with other dioceses, it forms the Catholic church. This idea of dioceses being truly the church is important for the future because it bears within it the seeds of pastoral sensitivity to local issues and a proper balance in the relationship with Rome. Nobody is more important in these matters than the bishop. He is a member of the college of bishops, of that group responsible for sanctifying, teaching, and ruling the church. Thus we speak of the collegiality of bishops, of their responsibility to maintain communion and fellowship between the various dioceses (particular churches) throughout the world. The head of that college is the bishop of Rome, usually called the pope. In the first few fractious centuries of Christian history, when there was painful division between the particular churches, the bishop of Rome emerged as the focus of unity and communion in the universal church. Even today this remains the key element in the ministry of the bishop of Rome—to foster communion and fellowship between the particular churches (dioceses) throughout the world. The pope does not govern each diocese—that is the task of the local bishop. Rather the pope personifies the universality of the church, and he must ensure that the necessary bonds of faith, hope, and charity are maintained and fostered among the particular churches. It is one of the great tragedies of Christian history that this very office has itself become the main focus of disputes and divisions. One of the most important tasks facing the Catholic church today is to work out the proper relationship between Rome and the particular churches in dioceses throughout the world. This relationship has evolved historically, and we can look forward to further evolution in the future. Such developments are important for the Catholic church itself and are of crucial significance for its relationships with other Christian traditions.

A bishop must sanctify, teach, and rule the particular church that he oversees. It is easy to understand, then, why bishops are generally conservative. They must conserve the teaching of the apostles, which has been handed down from one generation to the next, and they must maintain the bonds of communion with other dioceses both near and far. Such demanding tasks would make one naturally suspicious of changing fashions and mores that tend to be ephemeral and limited to specific geographical areas. But bishops must also lead their people to new horizons of faith and practice. They could learn much about this from the leaders of the church in the first century who adapted the church's life and language to varied religious, intellectual, and political contexts. Today we speak of this as inculturation. The church will always have need of leaders who can speak the ancient message with new and creative voices.

Priests/presbyters

The people we traditionally call priests should more exactly be called "priests of the presbyteral order," since the category of priest also includes bishops. The Greek word *presbyteros* means "elder." To be a priest in the presbyteral order means that one is ordained to take a role of leadership in the community as a minister of word and sacrament. The reality of leader or elder is best expressed in the role of parish priest or pastor. The diocese of which the bishop is the "overseer" is subdivided into parishes in which the parish priest has the responsibility to preach the word and celebrate the sacraments. Sometimes he might be supported in this by curates or assistant pastors.

Priests have a crucial role to play in the life of the church but, since the Second Vatican Council, important questions have been raised about the very nature of the priesthood. Vatican II can quite properly be spoken of as the "council of bishops" because it focused on the centrality of the episcopal ministry and renewed and amplified the life of bishops in the church. Similarly the role of the laity and those who live under religious vows was acknowledged and deepened. But the document on the life of priests/presbyters, *Presbyterorum Ordinis,* did not have the same cutting edge. As a result the new theological underpinning of bishops, laity, and those living under religious vows was not replicated for the presbyterate. We have been living with the implications of this ever since as the new relationship between the priests/presbyters and the other groups are still being worked out. Priests entered Vatican II as the very heartbeat of the church around whom everything was organized and structured; they emerged from the council into

a different ecclesial setting where some old certainties were beginning to wear very thin. Tension, misunderstanding, and
downright hostility have characterized many relationships as
priests ceaselessly ask themselves: Who are we? What is our
role?

Vatican II did not give theologically significant answers to
these questions but it opened up a whole range of other issues
that posed seemingly endless questions for the presbyterate:
What is the new relationship with the laity? What are the pri-
orities in ministry? What exactly should one do from day to
day? The renewal initiated at the council found its focus for
those living under religious vows in a rediscovery of the
charisms of their founders; for the baptized there were newly
emerging theologies giving people a real sense of the meaning
of their baptism; for bishops there was an edifying vision of
their apostolic calling; but for priests there was little but the
chilly words of the code of canon law. No matter how much
significance one attaches to law, it is not the most potent moti-
vating force for creating the future; theologies that both challenge and affirm the presbyterate are required if the priests of
the future are to discover who they are in the life of the baptismal community.

Christian priesthood means nothing apart from Jesus who
is called the Christ. Two thousand years ago he preached the
dawning reign of God. He wasn't a member of the priestly
caste of his time but that didn't stop him from preaching the
good news, healing the sick, bringing liberty to captives, comforting the brokenhearted, bringing new sight to the blind,
and building a self-identity that was forged in his interaction
with the one he called "Abba" and in his encounter with
friends and foes on the highways and byways of Galilee.
Through prayer, reflection, and human encounter Jesus discovered the divine depths of life. All Christians are asked to
follow him on this path but priests have a particularly signifi-

cant role to play. They are asked to preside at the liturgical gatherings of the community, to preach the gospel, and to lead people through prayer and sacrament to an ever deeper encounter with the divine depths of our lives. These are demanding tasks. Nobody could even begin to fulfill them in a meaningful way without serious dedication to prayer, reading, and self-reflection. Without these a priest's ministry is likely to spiral into a decline of empty repetitions, hollow encounters, and pious rhetoric.

One shouldn't conclude, however, that there is only one way of being a priest in the tradition of Jesus of Nazareth. There are as many ways of living priestly life as there are priests in the world. Every priest has the right to forge his identity in the context in which he finds himself. Some will want to live in a countercultural manner through wearing distinctive dress, living frugally, and standing apart from many social activities. Others prefer to be more like a leaven in the world—alive and active but not readily distinguishable from everybody else. One way or the other, the task is always to proclaim the dawning reign of God as Jesus did.

That which distinguishes Christian faith from other religions is belief in the Trinity and the incarnation. Think about these wonderful doctrines for a moment. In God's own life there is relationship; God is one but not solitary. In the incarnation God embraced humanity in all its beauty and wickedness and began to transform it from within. These doctrines, the very heartbeat of Christianity, should tell us much about priesthood. The priest's life should, like that of the triune God, be characterized by life-giving and sustaining relationships and, like Christ, the priest should be immersed in the tangled human world of good and evil, hope and despair, life and death. Priests must try to wander around the sacred spaces in the world and in the soul; they should visit the corners of brokenness and emptiness and yet hear the call to transcendence;

they should hope against hope and, in a very traditional language, they should know the depth of their own sinfulness and the breadth of divine love. And then, in the tradition of Christ himself, their words might indeed be redemptive and salvific.

Sacrifice is one of the defining aspects of all religions. Priesthood and sacrifice are inseparable. The priest is the one who offers the sacrifice, the altar is the place where the offering is made, and the victim is that which is offered. In many ancient pagan religions the firstborn was sacrificed to the gods—originally this was a human, later an animal or the first fruits of the harvest. In the Jewish tradition the priests oversaw the temple sacrifices. But it is noteworthy that the early Christians did not adopt the language and symbols of the Jewish priesthood. The first believers attached numerous titles to Jesus but they were very slow to speak of him as the new high priest. This language was developed in the letter to the Hebrews. The letter was written after the destruction of the temple in 70 AD, and it addressed a real issue for the Jewish Christians who had remained faithful to the temple sacrifices—what is the meaning of priesthood once the temple had disappeared? Clearly there was a problem, since Jesus was no priest in the ordinary Jewish sense. He hadn't been born of the right stock, and not only had he not been a priest in the Jerusalem temple but he had attacked it with some fury. As a result the letter to the Hebrews reinterpreted the meaning of the priesthood. Christ is spoken of as the priest and the victim since he sacrificed his own life on a new altar—the cross. Therefore Christians came to understand Christ as the new high priest, the one who offers the sacrifice, and is the victim, for he was the one who was offered. Thus the ancient tradition of sacrifice is given a new interpretation—the demand for self-sacrifice.

A key element in the renewal of priestly life will be self-sac-

rifice. The great temptation is toward comfortable bachelor-
hood. Such a lifestyle has little to say to anyone. It needs to be
thrown into serious question before it quenches the spirit of
the gospel. One way of rekindling this spirit is to withdraw to
the edge, the threshold, the desert. The encounter with life on
the edge, the periphery, the margins, remains the key to unleashing the powers of renewal in the lives of individuals and
in the lives of great institutions like the churches. Creativity
emerges from the margins. Artists, writers, philosophers, and
mystics all go to the edge, the margins of their experience, and
from there they interrogate the presumptions upon which our
world is built. Priests need to withdraw to the edge too in
order to revisit the wellsprings that nourish Christian faith.
They can do so by participating in a serious retreat, going on
sabbatical, or volunteering for work in impoverished communities at home or abroad. Such experiences, which often demand great self-sacrifice, are the food of the soul.

This theology of sacrifice found its most powerful expression in the rule concerning priestly celibacy. The tradition of
celibate priests has a long and rich history in the Catholic
church. Only those with a very biased view of things would
question the contribution that a celibate priesthood has made
to prayer and pastoral care, to missionary outreach and
Christian living. But the rise of modern psychology and the
emergence of the sexual revolution, which have engrossed
Western civilization since the 1960s, naturally throw such a
tradition into question. We now know far more than previous
generations did about friendship and emotional maturity, sex-
uality and personal identity, childhood experiences and problems in later life, homosexuality and homophobia, child sexual abuse and manipulative relationships. The world of sexual
innocence has been shattered. Things will never be the same
again. It is as if a still pond of water has been upset and all the
material that rested at the bottom has begun to rise to the sur-

face. The reality of child sexual abuse perpetrated by some
clergy and religious has changed people's perception of celibacy. It probably was the case that most people could never understand celibacy as an option for life and so they elevated
those who chose such a path onto a pedestal of purity and innocence that they didn't share. Now they know that those who
try to live celibate lives are as sexually and emotionally complicated as everybody else.

The celibate priesthood has a future since its ranks include
people of extraordinary emotional maturity, generosity, and
other-centeredness. But there is no reversing the insights of
psychology or the power of the sexual revolution. We know
that life cannot be lived in a humane way without intimacy
and friendship, that celibacy can be an escape mechanism
from these realities, but that it can also be lived in a way that
overcomes isolation and fear. As ever, it is probably a good
idea to look back to the Scriptures. The life of Jesus makes no
sense apart from very particular people: Mary, Martha, and
Lazarus, who lived in the poor village of Bethany, the beloved
disciple, and the other women and men whom he encountered
on the way. Wherever the church learned in later times to mis-
trust the value of friendship and intimacy, it certainly wasn't
from deep reflection on the life of Jesus of Nazareth.

Deacons

The third order of the three holy orders is the diaconate. It has
had a troubled history. For a thousand years prior to Vatican II
there were no permanent deacons in the Catholic church.
Throughout the first millennium of the Christian era, the
priesthood grew in stature and power to such an extent that
the diaconate became all but obsolete. In the second millennium the diaconate became nothing more than a stepping stone
to the priesthood. Before one could be ordained a priest in the
presbyteral order one had first to be ordained a deacon. This

remains the case today. But Vatican II introduced an important reform when it set in motion the process by which the permanent diaconate was restored in the life of the church. Thus today we speak of the transitional diaconate (those who will shortly be ordained as priests) and the permanent diaconate (those who will remain deacons for the rest of their lives).

The Greek word *diakonia* means "service." Thus deacons are called to serve the Christian community. They do this through preaching the word of God, baptizing new members of the church, assisting at marriages, presiding at funerals, and reaching out to those in need. The re-establishment of the permanent diaconate in the Catholic church has given new life to this ancient ministry. The fact that married men can be ordained to this ministry means that it opens the door to ordination for many who were previously excluded.

Ordination ceremonies

The various rites of ordination are among the most potent rituals of the Catholic church. The rites were revised in light of the Second Vatican Council. Through the prayer of consecration and the laying on of hands by the bishop, a member of the Christian community is ordained to one of the three orders.

The three ceremonies have much in common. Candidates for the diaconate and presbyterate are presented to the bishop and the assembly by a relevant person (maybe the parish priest or a representative from the seminary where the candidate trained). The bishop asks if they have been found worthy, and the assembly expresses its consent. This latter aspect is interesting, for the reality is that the community is not involved in making any judgment on the suitability of the candidate. But the survival of this ancient tradition in the rite is welcome since the possibility remains that at some time in the future the community might again have a more significant role in

choosing its own leaders. At any rate this is a good time in the
rite for someone who knows the candidate to speak of his
Christian maturity and suitability for the ministry upon which
he is about to embark; this obviously implies that if the candidate is immature or unsuitable then he should not be presented for ordination.

In the case of the episcopate, the one to be ordained is presented to the assembled bishops, and the community and the
apostolic mandate (a letter from the pope approving the individual for ordination as bishop of the particular diocese) is
read. In all three rites, the candidate is then examined in public before the gathered community. Then he lies prostrate
while the community intercedes for the gift of the Holy Spirit.
This is followed by the key moment in the rite with the laying
on of hands and the prayer of consecration. Since bishops and
presbyters are given a share in the priesthood of Christ, they
are anointed with chrism (deacons are not so anointed because they are not ordained to the priesthood). Finally, the
newly ordained are presented with symbols and insignia proper to their office—a bishop receives the gospels, a ring, a mitre,
and a staff; a presbyter is clothed in a chasuble and stole and
presented with bread and wine; a deacon is vested with a dal-
matic and stole and is given the gospels. The rite closes with
the kiss of peace.

These sacramental rituals clearly constitute rites of passage
through which an individual is bestowed with a new office in
the Christian community. Given the importance of these ministers in the life of the community, it is surely welcome that
most ordinations now take place in an active parish church and,
in the case of the episcopal rite, in the local cathedral.

A priestly community

One cannot understand the episcopate, presbyterate, and diaconate without the community of believers. However small or

disorganized, however persecuted or comfortable, however strong or weak, however traditional or prophetic, however active or dormant, the community of believers is the primordial reality in Christianity. All else only makes sense as emerging from and existing for the community. The single greatest threat to Christian faith in the Western world is the growing privatization of life. Homes are becoming zones of seclusion; worse, the inhabitants want it that way. The withdrawal into our living rooms, where the television can become the key access to the world, inevitably fragments the communal world that we once inhabited. The onslaught of the internet and cyberspace will offer opportunities for new types of cyber-communities where one's neighbor will not be defined geographically in terms of traditional space and time but through cyberspace and time. In this world of technological revolution, sacramental space is squeezed and the interaction of community, religious belief, and ritual is thrown into serious question. Whatever the merits of privatization in business and commerce, it is a fatal flaw in religious sensibility. In such a world it is difficult to speak of the true meaning of Christianity; people are probably happy enough to receive the body of Christ but they have little taste for that same body as encountered in the community of believers.

The church is properly understood to be the people of God, the body of Christ, and the temple of the Holy Spirit. Such an understanding should awaken in each member of the church a sense of his or her baptismal dignity. But sadly this has seldom been the case. The ministries of bishops, priests, and deacons evolved over the first few centuries of Christian history. In time the priesthood became the most important office in the Catholic church. As ever, the great temptation was to abuse power, to become one who dominated and around whom everything else revolved. Down through history, the dominance of the priest continued to grow to such an extent that one could be forgiven for thinking that in the post-Tridentine church the community existed for the priest. But the Second Vatican Council gave fresh impetus to an old doctrine—that all the baptized share in the priesthood of Christ. Thus part of the task of the future is to awaken Christian communities to their priestly character through fostering charisms and new ministries to give expression to this priestly dimension.

It is easy to be clear about what this does not mean. It does not mean that everyone who is baptized is also ordained as a priest. The ministerial priesthood of word and sacrament remains clearly distinct. But it does mean that all baptized Christians are called to share in the priesthood of Christ. They can do so in different ways but the ultimate goal is that the charisms freely bestowed by the Spirit of God should be placed at the service of all. From a Christian perspective, charisms or gifts are not just personal talents, they are intended for building up the community. They vary enormously and are literally innumerable, but to give a flavor of how gifted the Christian community is, here are just a few: consoling the bereaved, healing the sick, comforting the lonely, encouraging the downcast, embracing poverty, reaching out to the addicted, being celibate, counseling, praying, leading, forgiving, teaching, believing, hoping, loving. These charisms are present in abundance; it is the task of a priestly community to affirm them, harness them, and challenge those who have been so blessed to put their gifts at the service of the Christian community. This has been one of our great failures to date. With the clericalization of ministry, the baptized have lost all sense of their priestly character.

The Christian priestly communities that emerge in the cities of the future will be countercultural, creating sacred sacramental spaces in the midst of urban anonymity, sowing the seeds of the kingdom of God in soil that appears hostile, disturbing the cozy conscience of the consumer. There are a few certainties about such communities: they will not be a "one man show" where all power is vested in the parish priest. The great temptation for the priest is to think that he is on his own and then to lapse into either frustration (where nothing gets done) or dictatorship (where virtually everyone gets alienated). Instead he must cultivate a sense of shared responsibility. In the future there will be a plurality of ministries, and it is probably the case that we will have to imagine new structures apart from the parish to incarnate the church in the city. The best priests have always devoted their energies, wherever they found themselves, to building community; that task has not changed but it cannot be undertaken alone. The days of the priestly "lone ranger" are numbered.

The key question facing the church in the Western world today is not "who should be ordained?" but "what does it mean to be baptized?" Since Vatican II we have made a lot of mistakes in attempting to answer that question. We fell into the trap of equating lay participation/ministry with sanctuary ministry. Lectors (readers at Mass) and extraordinary ministers of the Eucharist became the be-all and end-all of lay participation. To reduce lay participation in the church to these very limited roles is essentially to empty it of all significance. It must be expanded to include parish catechists, family and bereavement counselors, chaplains (though maybe we need a different title) for schools and hospitals and prisons. When one adds to this all the tasks currently performed by priests but which have nothing directly to do with priestly ministry— from representation on school boards to organizing parish finances and, on a different level, from representing the church at international gatherings to staffing the Vatican's diplomatic corps—one can see that there is a lot to be done that need not be done by priests.

Is it true, as some commentators suggest, that there is a real hostility to change among the clergy? More important, is it true that younger clergy are even less interested in a new future than their older confrères? Priests need to realize that the days of lording it over the people are gone. What the church needs most of all today are people who can articulate the significance of Christian faith, who can speak a word of healing and hope, in a secular but broken world. It has little need of those who can only parrot doctrine and moral absolutes. The most important development in twentieth-century thought was the quantum leap whereby physicists moved from the world of Newtonian certainty to the unpredictable universe of subatomic physics. The Catholic church needs a quantum leap of faith to bring it to new horizons. While cherishing many of the things it holds dear, it needs to abandon some old attachments in the embrace of an unpredictable future. If its clergy are not up to this task then they risk being left behind in a lonely ghetto.

Conclusion

The priest has a crucial role to play in the life of every Christian community. As a minister of word and sacrament, he leads the assemblies of believers when they gather for their sacramental rituals. The great occupational hazard of such ministry is that repetition can sap the energy and insight that are so necessary in the leader of the assembly. A priest encounters people at critical threshold moments in their lives—birth, death, serious illness, marriage, and at times of reconciliation. He needs to develop a sensitivity for symbol and ritual so that his words and actions bring healing and hope into people's lives.

In chapter one we outlined the various ways in which a community could awaken a sense of the edge/threshold in sacramental celebrations, yet without doubt the priest is central to this process. He must act as a leader in this area because laypeople will not feel that they can take the initiative in sacramental renewal. A significant number in any parish may have worthwhile ideas about how to celebrate the sacraments more fruitfully as threshold experiences, yet their efforts are destined to founder without the good will and support of the priest.

A sacramental people needs to encounter, through word and symbol, those Christian realities that can give meaning and perspective to our lives. Simply, we need to experience our sacraments as thresholds. Our primitive forebears celebrated the transformations of the seasons and the cosmos and the passages of life and death. Woven into this rich tapestry of ritual and symbol is a narrative that demands that we embrace the thresholds that we constantly encounter in life. Remember, the threshold is a place of perspective and change, renewal and critique. Our sacraments will speak to the lives of those in our communities when they too become thresholds, truly doors that open onto the very life of God.

Contemporary life is weighed down by the demands of materialism and the fruits of a consumerism that only bequeathes isolation and anxiety. We have never been in such need of the renewing qualities of ritual, and a definitive responsibility lies with priests to awaken a sense of the edge/ threshold. The contemporary role of the church may well be to serve the needs of a society that is illiterate in the grammar of ritual and symbol. Of all the social institutions, it is the Catholic church that is competent in ritual; of all times, it is our era that begs such a proficiency.

PART IV

Being a Sacramental People

In this chapter we describe many different rituals. Some of the reflective texts used in these rituals can be found in the Appendix. Our intention is that parishes, schools, retreat teams, or other communities might adapt these texts and rituals to their own needs. We give a few suggestions as to their likely use but these are only broad guidelines. It is more important to use your imagination in adapting these ideas to your own context. Remember the basic premise of this book is that the key symbols of the sacraments are more powerful than we ordinarily believe, and that if we allow them to speak they could become a focus for renewal in the church. Interacting with symbols breathes new life into our faith because without them faith is little more than an intellectual claim, but through them it becomes incarnate and communal. The only way to see if this works is actually to try it. You might be surprised by what you discover. Remember to keep in mind the issues concerning rituals that were discussed in chapter one.

1. Landscapes and Seascapes

In this ritual we visit significant geographical sites that help to awaken a sense of life on the threshold. In the text that follows we mention hills, monasteries, wells, seashore, and tombs. The ritual is easily adapted for use in one or more of these locations. Ideally a group of participants should spend a day walking from one site to the other.

• *On the Mountaintop*
The participants gather in a circle facing inward.

Leader: Why have people always come to the mountaintop?
Down below on the plains and in the valleys life is familiar, routine, and often banal. In the city the streets are thronged and things move quickly. In our homes the television is ever present. In the car our space is cramped. In the workplace there is little time to do what we want.

But here on the mountaintop life is unfamiliar, different, and refreshing. The ascent can be slow and difficult yet we always struggle to the top to touch again the vast emptiness, to see again the distant horizons, to taste again the unfettered wind, to smell again the fragrant air, to hear again the sounds of silence.

Look around you. Touch the emptiness. Look at the horizons. Taste the wind. Smell the air. Listen to the silence.

Depending on the place and the amount of time available, the participants should now be given some time to wander freely. When the people regather they should form a circle again but this time facing outward. Then the following pieces of Scripture are read.

Reader 1: I lift up my eyes to the mountains:

From where shall come my help?
My help shall come from the Lord
Who made heaven and earth.
(Psalm 121)

Reader 2: Go up on the high mountain,
joyful messenger to Sion.
Shout with a loud voice
joyful messenger to Jerusalem.
Shout without fear
say to the towns of Judah
"Here is your God."
(Is 40:9)

Leader: The mountain is holy ground; it is sacred space. Moses encountered the Lord Yahweh on the mountaintop. Down below the people strayed, seduced by the lure of false gods. They forgot who they truly were and became immersed in the world and its attractions. They would have to learn over and over again to climb the mountain of the Lord and to seek God's ways. We too must visit these holy places to rediscover the truth of who we are as God's own people, a holy nation, a royal priesthood, a people set apart to sing the praises of God. Before we return to the valleys and plains, to the cities and the suburbs, to our cars and homes, we anoint one another with oil of gladness to strengthen us on life's journey.

Each participant is anointed with oil.

Leader: Remember that this is a holy place, remember who you are.

Participant: On the mountain God provides. (Gen 22:14)

The participants descend the hill or mountain. At a suitable location at the bottom they gather again in a circle.

Leader: Look again to the mountaintop. Remember this is a sacred place.

All recite or sing together:
The Lord is my shepherd,
I shall not want.
He makes me lie down in green pastures;
he leads me beside still waters;
he restores my soul.
He leads me in right paths for his name's sake.
Even though I walk through the darkest valley,
I fear no evil;
for you are with me;
your rod and your staff—they comfort me.
You prepare a table before me
in the presence of my enemies;
you anoint my head with oil;
my cup overflows.
Surely goodness and mercy shall follow me
all the days of my life,
and I shall dwell in the house of the Lord
my whole life long.

• At the Monastery

The people might gather in the vicinity of a living monastery or in the ruins of a long since extinct one.

Leader: When Samuel was a boy it was rare for God to speak in those days. Yet God called out to Samuel but the boy did not understand that God was calling him. When he heard his name being called he ran to Eli and said, "Here I am" because he did not understand. Then Eli told him the truth and when God called the third time Samuel replied, "Speak, Lord, your servant is listening." Then God spoke to Samuel and his life was never the same afterward.

Reader 1: When we are old enough we understand that sometimes we must let go of our plans and let God be the God of our future:

"Very truly, I tell you,

when you were younger,

you used to fasten your own belt

and to go wherever you wished.

But when you grow old,

you will stretch out your hands,

and someone else will fasten a belt around you

and take you where you do not wish to go." (Jn 21:18)

Leader: Look around you at these hallowed walls. This sacred place is replete with the memories of those who have left the world to journey into the mystery of the inner self, supported by a community of faith. Like Samuel these servants learned to listen to the voice of the spirit of God and relinquish the call of the spirit of the world.

Read: "The spirit of God and the spirit of the world."

Two readers are needed; one reads the spirit of the world and the other the spirit of God. In each case the spirit of the world comes first followed within a couple of seconds by the spirit of God; there is then a substantial pause (10-15 seconds) before moving on. Ideally the two readers should stand at opposite ends of the relevant space.

1. The spirit of the world says that externals are all important—looks, property, possessions. We are what we have.
2. The spirit of God says that our looks and appearance can be very deceptive. We must look into the heart, into the depth of life to see who we really are.

1. The spirit of the world says that life is a test, and success is everything. It abhors failure and disappointment.

2. The spirit of God says that failure can be more important than success. We can learn much even from the sad and more difficult times.

1. The spirit of the world says that the great problems—unemployment, ecology, violence—have nothing to do with us. We've just got to mind our own business.
2. The spirit of God says that we are responsible for everyone, everywhere, at all times. There are no strangers in God's eyes.

1. The spirit of the world says that love is about things going well, in accord with our plans.
2. The spirit of God says that love is about giving of ourselves, even when we feel that we cannot.

1. The spirit of the world says that there is no such thing as forgiveness because there is no such thing as sin.
2. The spirit of God says that forgiveness is the greatest reality that we know. We sin, we fail, yet we can be freed to go on.

1. The spirit of the world says that honesty and commitment are impossible and don't really exist.
2. The spirit of God says that honesty and commitment are the only things that really matter in the end.

1. The spirit of the world says that the sick and the disabled are not really alive. Sickness and disability are disastrous.
2. The spirit of God says that the sick and the disabled are often those who are most alive for they know their dependence; they know that life is not in their control.

1. The spirit of the world says that death is the end of life and proves that life is futile.
2. The spirit of God says that death is not the end of life because the great spirit present in us is not extinguished but transformed.

Leader: We have all made choices, and each in his or her way has listened to the call of God. We have been called as men or women and given the gifts and talents to answer the call of our baptism to become truly Christian.

Rituals should regenerate and give people new energy. There might be an opportunity now to use the rites of affirmation on pp. 139-143. These rites are intended to highlight the gifts of various adults within the community: women, men, priests. Each group (women, men, priests) is called forward separately. They go to the front of the group where they stand facing the leader/elders while the others remain seated. Then the texts are read aloud by the leader/elders. Immediately afterward they place an open Bible over the head of each individual and say: "God's word has been sown in your heart. You are God's word."

• Around the Well

Leader: Water is the source of all life, and it was through water that we entered a life of faith in Christ. When we revisit water we revisit the sacrament of our baptism, a sacrament that we may have long forgotten.

Read the following text. Two readers are required.

1. At the very dawn of creation God's Spirit breathed on the waters.
2. In the beginning God created the heavens and the earth. Now the earth was a formless void, there was darkness over the deep, and God's Spirit hovered over the water.

1. The waters of the great flood brought an end to sin and a new beginning of goodness.
2. I establish my covenant with you: no thing of flesh shall be swept away again by the waters of the flood. There shall be no flood to destroy the earth again.

1. Through the waters of the Red Sea God led Israel out of slavery.

2. Yahweh drove back the sea with a strong easterly wind all night, and he made dry land of the sea. The waters parted and the children of Israel went on dry ground right into the sea, walls of water to right and left of them.

1. In the waters of the Jordan Jesus was baptized by John and anointed with the Spirit.

2. Immediately afterwards the Spirit drove him out into the wilderness and he remained there for forty days, and was tempted by Satan. He was with the wild beasts, and the angels looked after him.

1. When Jesus hung on the cross blood and water flowed from his side.

2. When they came to Jesus, they found he was already dead, and so instead of breaking his legs one of the soldiers pierced his side with a lance and immediately there came out blood and water.

1. In baptism we were baptized with water in the name of the Father and of the Son and of the Holy Spirit.

2. When we were baptized in Christ Jesus we were baptized in his death; in other words, when we were baptized we went into the tomb with him and joined him in death, so that as Christ was raised from the dead by the Father's glory, we too might live a new life.

The leader sprinkles everyone with water saying:
You were baptized in the name of the Father and of the Son and of the Holy Spirit.

Alternatively people come forward and bless themselves with the water saying:
I believe in God the Father and the Son and the Holy Spirit.
As people are being sprinkled with water there is music or song.

The last part of the ritual is the renewal of baptismal promises:

Leader: Do you believe in God the creator of light and darkness, land and sea, heaven and earth, woman and man?
All: We do.

Leader: Do you cherish and protect the earth as God's creation?
All: We do.

Leader: Do you appreciate the gift of water, which endlessly
renews and sustains life?
All: We do.

Leader: Do you give thanks for the spring and the summer, the
sowing and the harvest, the sun and the moon, the wind
and the rain, the mountaintop and the seashore?
All: We do.

Leader: Do you believe that in the midst of a beautiful world
we, like Adam and Eve, live in the shadow of temptation
and evil?
All: We do.

Leader: Do you reject all that is evil?
All: We do.

Leader: Do you reject injustice, hatred, despair, and bigotry?
All: We do.

Leader: Do you reject all that undermines and destroys the gift
of life?
All: We do.

Leader: Do you believe that Jesus Christ is the savior of the
world?
All: We do.

Leader: Do you believe that Jesus died for us on Calvary and
was raised from the dead?
All: We do.

Leader: Do you believe that in baptism you became followers of Jesus?
All: We do.

Leader: Do you believe that when you were anointed with oil in baptism you received the gift of God's Spirit?
All: We do.

Leader: Do you believe that God's Spirit is present in humanity and that our destiny is to share fully in God's own life?
All: We do.

Leader: Do you accept the Christian identity that was given to you in your name at baptism?
All: We do.

Leader: Do you accept that your faith can only be lived with others in a Christian community?
All: We do.

Leader: Do you believe that the church, a community of saints and sinners, is the temple of God's presence in the world?
All: We do.

Leader: Do you take responsibility for the future well-being of the church?
All: We do.

Leader: Do you believe in the final triumph of Christ over sin, light over darkness, truth over lies, hope over despair, good over evil, and life over death?
All: We do.

Leader: Do you today, in the presence of fellow believers, confirm the meaning and implications of your baptism?
All: We do.

Leader: Do you now promise to live your life in accordance with the Christian faith, which we have professed together?
All: We do.

Leader: Then may God bless you and strengthen you as you bear witness to your faith.

• By the Shore

Leader: Many years ago our forebears cried out to God to save them from slavery. Moses led them out of Egypt to the shore of the Red Sea. Pursued by the Egyptian army the people feared death and cried out in their anguish "Better to work for the Egyptians than die in the wilderness." In the midst of unbelief God stretched back the waters and the people walked from the shore, from slavery, full of joy and faith in God.

There are dark places in life when we lose faith and in hopelessness would prefer to die in the wilderness of our own despair.

All present should be asked to take off their shoes and enter the water.

Leader: By the shores of the Sea of Galilee Jesus called his first disciples. Later they left the same shore and the wind rose and the storm lashed their modest fishing boat. Like their forebears at the shore of the Red Sea they despaired until Jesus calmed the waters and asked them "Where is your faith?"

In the midst of the crises, temptations, turmoils, and sufferings of modern life, we may ask: "Where is our God?" Our God says: "Where is your faith?"

Once after his death, Christ beckoned his disciples in from the Sea of Galilee. There they were filled with faith in the risen Christ. Look now at the sea and remember your faith in the Christ who saves and in the God who first spoke to Moses saying: "I have observed the misery of my people who are in Egypt...I know their sufferings and I have come down to deliver them."

Through the waters of the Red Sea and the waters of our baptism and from the shores of the Sea of Galilee, we are called to a discipleship of faith. Just as Christ demanded of his disciples by the shore, so it is demanded of you today:

As the following text is read to each person they are invited to walk in from the sea:

(Name) when you were young
you walked where you liked
but when you are old
you will be taken where you would rather not go.

• Visiting a Tomb or Graveyard

Leader: It is part of the rhythm of human life that something must die before new life can begin. Here in this place of dying and death we are reminded of the need to let go of those memories that prevent us from experiencing new life in Christ. Life can bring us to places of great hurt and tragedy, and these experiences can hold us bound in anger and resentment. Human life is wounded, broken, and at times torn apart, but just as we were baptized into Christ's death so too we were baptized into new life with him. Easter tells us that we are called to live a life of sacrifice, and so we must learn to let go of that which prevents us from experiencing the fullness of Christian life.

The following text, or something similar might be used:

Lord God, help me to let go.
Life is an endless process of letting go;
In our birth we had to let go of the security of our mother's womb and emerge into a strange world;
In adolescence we let go of the innocence of childhood;
All of us have to let go of home: parents must let go of their children, and children must let go of their parents;

Throughout life as we grow and mature we must continually let go of opinions, jobs, good health, and ultimately of
the idea that we are in control.
And, of course, in death we must let go of those we love.
Between womb and tomb life is an endless process of letting go.
Come, Holy Spirit, help me to let go so that even when the
letting go is tearful and sad it will awaken me to the mystery and wonder of life.
Life is the greatest gift we have received, and we must in the
end let go of this gift.
We must let go of the past to let God be the God of the future.

*A scriptural text for this rite can be taken from any of the passion
narratives and it is important that these texts play a central role to
stress the paschal nature of this dying in Christ. The shadow of the
words of St. Paul should envelop this place; "when we were baptized in Christ Jesus we were baptized in his death"(Rom 6:3). One
possibility then is to read the text of Ecclesiastes 3:1–8:*

For everything there is a season, and a time for every matter under heaven:
a time to be born, and a time to die;
a time to plant, and a time to pluck up what is planted;
a time to kill, and a time to heal;
a time to break down, and a time to build up;
a time to weep, and a time to laugh;
a time to mourn, and a time to dance;
a time to throw away stones, and a time to gather stones together;
a time to embrace, and a time to refrain from embracing;
a time to seek, and a time to lose;
a time to keep, and a time to throw away;

a time to tear, and a time to sew;
a time to keep silence, and a time to speak;
a time to love, and a time to hate;
a time for war, and a time for peace.

If the group are visiting a particular grave they might gather around it and recite the following text:

We are not afraid of dying to the old,
We are not afraid of giving birth to what is new,
We are not afraid of planting,
We are not afraid of uprooting what has been planted,
We are not afraid of searching,
We are not afraid of keeping or throwing away,
We are not afraid of tears or mourning,
We are not afraid of laughter.

Finally it should be noted that some soft singing or humming in the background can be very evocative.

2. Reconciliation service

Parts of the following texts could be used in the celebration of rite two of the sacrament of reconciliation. Ideally those who attend this service should sit in a circle. There should be two lecterns within the circle facing one another. Suitable music or songs can easily be woven into this service.

Leader: To be Christian is to be a member of a community of saints and sinners. In this community we often fail to live up to the meaning of our baptism and to live out what the Eucharist demands of us. Let us listen to God's word as it speaks to us today.

A couple of suitable Scripture texts should now be read or the following texts from St. Paul might be used. There should be two readers reciting the texts alternatively with a short pause between each one. The two readers should stand at the two lecterns.

1. The word of God cuts more finely than a double-edged sword. It cuts between the marrow and the bone so that the truth can emerge.
2. What we preach is Christ crucified; a scandal for Jews and folly for Greeks, but for us who believe, the wisdom and glory of God. For God's foolishness is wiser than human wisdom, and God's weakness is stronger than human strength.

1. It is when I am weak that I am strong, for I feel the power of Christ shining through my human weakness.
2. I, Paul, appointed by God to be an apostle, send greetings to the church of God in Corinth, to the holy people of Jesus Christ who are called to take their place among all the saints everywhere. May God our Father and the Lord Jesus Christ send you grace and peace.

1. Nothing can ever come between us and the love of God

made visible in Christ Jesus our Lord. No angel, no power, no division, no fear can ever separate us from the love of God.

2. The blessing cup that we bless is a communion with the blood of Christ, and the bread that we break is a communion with the body of Christ. Because there is only one loaf means that we, though many, are one body because we all share the one loaf and the one cup.

1. Love is always patient and kind, it is never jealous. Love is never boastful or conceited, it is never rude or selfish. Love takes no pleasure in other people's sins but delights in the truth. It is always ready to excuse, to trust, to hope, and to endure whatever comes.

2. Are you people in Galatia mad? Are you going to surrender the power of the Spirit and become slaves again? Surely you realize that Christ died for you and that you are now free?

1. We are only earthenware jars that hold this treasure, to make it clear that such an overwhelming power comes from God and not from us. We are in difficulties on all sides but never fear; we see no answer to our problems but never despair.

2. I thank my God each time I think of you and every time I pray for you, I pray with joy.

To help those assembled to reflect on their sinfulness the following text might be used.

Voice 1: Bless me, Father, for I have sinned; it is three weeks since my last confession.

Voice 2: It might be a month, a year, ten years, but we all need to speak about our real problems, our fears, our real failures. There is nothing worse in life than carrying great burdens for years. We need to be released, to be healed, to be forgiven.

Voice 1: I cursed.

Voice 2: Yes, I use some bad language but that is not cursing in the true sense. To curse is the opposite of to praise. We should give praise and thanks at all times; praise God for the wonder of creation; thank God and our forebears for the gift of life; dance for joy before the rainbow, the sea, the sky, and the stars. But instead I find myself cursing my luck and I forget to give praise and thanks.

Voice 1: I stole.

Voice 2: I've never really stolen anything significant—or have I? I suppose that I've often stolen the wonder from people's lives by my moodiness. I've stolen others' dignity by refusing to acknowledge their value, their independence. I've stolen my own beauty by not treasuring the gift of my own life.

Voice 1: I didn't say my prayers.

Voice 2: Usually I just forget them. I remember to pray when I need something or I am stuck in a rut. Now that I have some time to think I should reflect about things. I have family and friends. My table is bountiful and my home warm. I can see the sunrise and the sunset and I can hear the wind and the rain. I am alive. However in my ordinary life I forget these things. To pray is to truly remember.

Voice 1: I lied.

Voice 2: We all tell the odd white lie. Yet it's easy to get into the habit of lying. I lie when I fail to see the truth in another person. The truth is that everyone is precious in God's eyes. Do I ever ask myself whether what I've heard is true or not? To speak the truth is difficult and demanding.

Voice 1: I missed Mass.

Voice 2: I know I should go because it's an obligation. But it

can be very tedious and repetitive, and I am easily distracted. Yet I am part of the great story that is being told. When
the bread is broken so too I experience brokenness and difficulty. When the wine is poured so too am I asked to give
of myself to the rest of the world. When the community
gathered I wasn't present. I missed Mass and I missed out
on part of who I am.

*It is the common experience of Christians that they sin again after
celebrating sacramental reconciliation. In order to strengthen
them for the journey that lies ahead the following text might be
read. Two readers are needed, one reads the spirit of the world and
the other the spirit of God. In each case the spirit of the world
comes first followed within a couple of seconds by the spirit of
God; there is then a substantial pause (10-15 seconds) before
moving on. The two readers should stand at the two lecterns.*

1. The spirit of the world says that externals are all important—looks, property, possessions. We are what we have.
2. The spirit of God says that our looks and appearance can be
   very deceptive. We must look into the heart, into the depth
   of life to see who we really are.

1. The spirit of the world says that life is a test, and success is
   everything. It abhors failure and disappointment.
2. The spirit of God says that failure can be more important
   than success. We can learn much even from the sad and
   more difficult times.

1. The spirit of the world says that the great problems—unemployment, ecology, violence—have nothing to do with us.
   We've just got to mind our own business.
2. The spirit of God says that we am responsible for everyone,
   everywhere, at all times. There are no strangers in God's eyes.

1. The spirit of the world says that love is about things going
   well, in accord with our plans.

2. The spirit of God says that love is about giving of ourselves, even when we feel that we cannot.

1. The spirit of the world says that there is no such thing as forgiveness because there is no such thing as sin.

2. The spirit of God says that forgiveness is the greatest reality that we know. We sin, we fail, yet we can be freed to go on.

1. The spirit of the world says that honesty and commitment are impossible and don't really exist.

2. The spirit of God says that honesty and commitment are the only things that really matter in the end.

1. The spirit of the world says that the sick and the disabled are not really alive. Sickness and disability are disastrous.

2. The spirit of God says that the sick and the disabled are often those who are most alive for they know their dependence; they know that life is not in their control.

1. The spirit of the world says that death is the end of life and proves that life is futile.

2. The spirit of God says that death is not the end of life because the great spirit present in us is not extinguished but transformed.

Leader: Because all of us are members of the baptized community, we will be anointed with chrism as a reminder of our baptism and confirmation. We received the Spirit of God in those sacraments, and this oil reminds us that we must continue to struggle to give that Spirit free reign in our lives.

All present should be anointed with oil while the minister says:

God's Spirit has been poured into our hearts. May you be strengthened to live in accord with the values of God's Spirit.

The service might conclude with these or similar words:

You are the salt of the earth,
you are the light of the world,
together we are the body of Christ.
As a baby you were baptized in Christ,
at seven years you were invited to eat
from the altar of God,
and later the church confirmed the gift of God's Spirit given
to you.
Go now from this holy place,
treasure in your heart the wonder of who you are,
and may the words you have heard here
ever echo in your mind.
You are the salt of the earth,
you are the light of the world,
together we are the body of Christ.

3. A Service of Healing

This ritual could include the formal anointing of the sick. Suitable music or songs can easily be woven into this service.

Leader: We are gathered as God's people in need of healing. Let us listen to God's word.

In each case a personal reflection comes first followed after a pause by a biblical quotation; there is then a further pause before moving on.

1. We are children of the earth, made of the same stuff as the stars. We are part of the beauty of the earth.
2. In the beginning God created the heavens and the earth. Now the earth was a formless void, there was darkness over the deep, and God's Spirit hovered over the water. God saw what God had made, and it was very good.

1. Think of the date you were born, the joy of your parents, family, neighbors, and friends. Imagine yourself as a baby.
2. Before I formed you in the womb I knew you, before you came to birth I consecrated you.

1. Recall in your own mind the various places you've lived. Think of the houses, the places—go into each of them in your mind.
2. Wherever you go, I will go, wherever you live I will live.

1. Think of a couple of really happy moments in your life. Treasure them in your heart.
2. I want you to be happy, always happy in the Lord; I repeat, what I want is your happiness.

1. Allow moments of suffering and pain to enter your mind. They are part of who we are.
2. Come to me all you who labor and are overburdened, and I will give you rest. For my yoke is easy and my burden is light.

1. Who are the people who accompany you? family, spouse, children, neighbors, friends? Look at their faces now.
2. Did not our hearts burn within us as he talked to us on the road and explained the Scriptures to us.... and their eyes were opened and they recognized him in the breaking of the bread.

1. What do you hope for? What are your greatest expectations, your cherished dreams?
2. What we suffer in this life can never be compared to the glory that is yet to be revealed.

1. Where will it all end? What will happen in the future?
2. I saw a new heaven and a new earth.... Then I heard a loud voice call from above: now I am making the whole of creation new.

Leader: We are a eucharistic people on our way to God's kingdom. But on this journey we need support and healing.

Reader:
In the Eucharist bread is taken, blessed, broken,
and given.
In life we are taken, blessed, broken, and given.
The priest takes the bread in his hands and blesses it during the eucharistic prayer;
then he breaks it, and it is given to us
as the body of Christ.
Through our birth and baptism we are taken into God's hands;
as the bread is taken, so too are we.
In life we are blessed by family, friends, love, and joy;
as the bread is blessed, so too are we.
We are broken by failure, sin, pain, and heartbreak;
as the bread is broken, so too are we.

In death we are given back to the mystery
from which we came;
as the bread is given, so too are we.
When we take, bless, break, and give bread
to one another,
we believe the Lord to be especially present
in our midst.
But we must learn to accept that in his memory
we will be taken, blessed, broken, and given
for the life of the world.

If there is only a small number of people present the leader should invite them all to place one hand on the shoulder of each person while a member of the group says:

You are not afraid of dying to the old,
You are not afraid of giving birth to what is new,
You are not afraid of planting,
You are not afraid of uprooting what has been planted,
You are not afraid of searching,
You are not afraid of keeping or throwing away,
You are not afraid of tears or mourning,
You are not afraid of laughter.

If there is a large number of people present a priest should lay hands on each individual while saying:
May you receive healing and strength to face life's difficulties.

Once the participants are seated again the following reflection is read.

Lord God help me to let go.
Life is an endless process of letting go;
In our birth we had to let go of the security of
our mother's womb and emerge into a strange world;
In adolescence we let go of the innocence of childhood;
All of us have to let go of home: parents must let go of their

children, and children must let go of their parents:
Throughout life as we grow and mature we must continually let go of opinions, jobs, good health, and ultimately of the idea that we are in control.
And, of course, in death we must let go of those we love.
Between womb and tomb life is an endless process of letting go.
Come, Holy Spirit, help me to let go so that even when the letting go is tearful and sad it will awaken me to the mystery and wonder of life.
Life is the greatest gift we have received, and in the end we must let go of this gift.
We must let go of the past to let God be the God of the future.

The community should often be reminded of the links between baptism, Eucharist, and healing. During services like these is a good time to renew baptismal promises. The text on pp. 97-99 could be used.

The service should close with a blessing.

4. Marriage

Given the nature of the sacrament of marriage the couple should be encouraged to plan the ceremony in some detail. Everything possible should be done to highlight the significance of the mutual giving of consent. The statement form should be used, and ideally the couple should face the congregation. It should also be made clear to those involved that they do not have to follow particular traditions which are not part of the marriage rite. Thus the bride and groom might walk in a procession together that might also include some relatives. The law demands that there be two witnesses; there can be other bridesmaids and groomsmen but they are not formally witnesses of the marriage.

The couple could also compose some introductory words and reflections for use during the ceremony.

• *Introduction*
One of the witnesses might introduce the ceremony as follows:
> N. and N. you are here today in this sacred place to exchange the vows of your love for each other. We are here as your family and friends to support you as you wed. In the presence of God we will witness the promise of your love.

• *Candles*
Sometimes it is customary for the bride and bridegroom to light two candles before the rite of marriage. Afterward a flame is taken from each of these candles and a single candle is lit as a sign of the unity of marriage. Alternatively the parents of the bride and bridegroom can be asked to light these two candles with this text:
> It was from our marriage that we gave you life. May you both give birth to another generation and may you be blessed with hope and happiness.

When the couple light the single candle they could use this text:

We thank God for the gift of life and the gift of love.

• *Giving consent*
*The amount of time that it takes to exchange marital vows is very
short. In order to give people time to reflect on the significance of
what is happening, there should be some music or song or a spoken
reflection after giving consent. These words might be spoken:*

May you know joy in each other's company,
and may your love carry you through the years ahead.

May your friends be plentiful and your table bountiful,
and may God's face smile upon your home.

May laughter and pleasure be with you always,
and may you grow old in the warmth of your embrace.

May compassion and understanding accompany you,
and through forgiveness may your love turn to gold.

*If the exchange of rings and other tokens takes place, this should
be mutual.*

• *Prayer of thanksgiving*
*The couple should be encouraged to compose their own prayer.
Here is an example:*

> We give thanks for our parents
> and for the gift of life;
> for their sacrifice,
> protection, and a thousand hugs.

> We give thanks for our family,
> for fights and forgiveness,
> for memories, too many to mention
> and presents at Christmastime.

> We give thanks for our friends,
> for generosity and loyalty,

for laughter and sorrow,
and secrets kept.

We give thanks to God
for the waters of baptism;
for Jesus' self-sacrifice
and the Spirit of love.

In thanksgiving, we pray that we may be
as generous and as kind as you are.
and may our marriage strengthen us
all the days of our life
To be truly Christian in faith, hope, and love.

5. Death of an Infant

The most difficult pastoral situation of all is the death of an infant. The official rites of the church are very helpful at this time. Here we suggest some texts and symbols that might be of some benefit. Symbols are very important at times such as these when our words begin to flounder. The priest or other minister should encourage some of those present to read some of the texts.

• *Candles*

Leader: After Jesus had died, the disciples hid in the upper room. Like us, they were filled with doubt and despair in the face of untimely death. They huddled together murmuring their confusion and whispering their loss. It was to such a group that God sent the Spirit at Pentecost to comfort their sorrow and sow understanding amid confusion. The Spirit came in tongues of fire and as these candles are lit we ask God to send his Spirit to those who mourn today. These candles will be given to N. and N. (parents). May they be filled with the Spirit and believe that N., who died in Christ, will live forever.

The candles can be blessed and then lit. If appropriate, those gathered can be invited to take a candle home with them.

• *Water*

Reader: Before N. was born he/she was nurtured and sustained in the womb. We celebrate a short life lived in the waters of warmth and comfort. It was a life free from sorrow or pain, cradled only in love and joyful expectation. Like our love for N., Christ's love for us is never ending.

For a baptized infant:

In his/her baptism N. was reborn into the gift of everlasting life. N. was born into our embrace and our love and now he/she has been reborn into the arms of God's love.

For an infant who died before baptism:
> N. was born into our embrace and our love, and now, through death, he/she is reborn into the mystery of the love and mercy of God.

The priest then invites everyone present to bless themselves with water saying:
> We have been baptized into the mystery of everlasting life.
Those gathered can be invited to take some of the blessed water home with them.

• *Clothes*
Reader: N., we held out for you the promise of life, yet unexpectedly this gift has been taken away from us all. We had arrangements made for you and a place prepared in our home. We had clothes to keep you warm, toys to keep you happy, and a treasure of unspoken hopes and wishes. We wanted so much to care for you and prove our love. And so we wrap you in these clothes to keep you on your journey.

At this point the parents can wrap the infant in the clothes prepared saying:
> May you find the care we had prepared for you with all the saints in heaven.

If the parents find it comforting and an expression of their care, items may be placed in the coffin. The prayers of the faithful could accompany these.

• *The Lord's Prayer and the sign of peace*
Leader: In these terrible hours we have wrung our hands in anguish and our eyes have been washed with tears of sorrow. Within this death there is an emptiness difficult to fathom and a silence that baffles our sense. It is with a weak voice that we cry to God and ask for the spirit of strength and acceptance.
All: *All recite the Lord's Prayer.*

The priest then blesses all present:
Come to me, all you who labor and are overburdened, and I
will give you rest.

The rite could conclude with the sign of peace.

*Parents and others bereaved should be encouraged to write about
their thoughts and feelings. Such reflections might be used on occasions such as anniversaries. Here is one example:*

A mother's prayer on the death of her child
The land of our promise was populated with every kind of
hope for you,
every kind of wish for your life.
We had imagined who you would be like;
handsome and witty, thought your father,
practical and purposeful like your mother, I claimed.
Little child, why did you go away
before you had learned to live at all?

They said you'd keep us up all night,
that things would never be the same again.
Friends hoped to see your father
with a diaper in his hand,
with tired eyes and a sleepy head.
The fun we'd have putting you to bed.
Little child, you have turned our world upside down,
our tired eyes and our sleepy heads.

Your father enthused about the talents
on his side of the family.
You'd be a professional, a doctor most likely!
I wondered what your ways would be like.
Would you be grumpy like your grandfather
or mellow and secretive like grandma?
The questions and questions that go 'round in my mind.

You are a mystery and a feast of answers
an unknown martyr, and an innocent victim
of the dark and terrible ways of this world.
One day this veil of mourning will be lifted
and we will be with you where you are now going.
Be there, N., to put your arms around us
For in you, little child, we have seen a glimpse of heaven.

• *At the graveside*
Reading: The empty tomb (Jn 20:1–10).

Leader: We would not have chosen to gather here today beside this empty grave, but at times like this we are forced to ponder the mysteries of life and death in Christ. The reading we have listened to tells us of the meaning of an empty grave. We look at this stark and lonely scene and our hearts, though like lead, are filled only with emptiness. In the story of the empty tomb, the other disciple, like us, did not want to look into an empty grave, afraid that he might only see death and hopelessness. But Peter went into the tomb and discovered not death but new life in the linen cloths gathered on the ground. N. has gone into the tomb and died with Christ, but let these cloths that he/she was wrapped in be given to you as a sign of his/her new life in Christ.

It is suggested that a special cloth that the infant was wrapped in be then given to the parents saying:
  Treasure this sacred cloth. N. is alive in Christ.

Comforting signs regarding death and new life can be revealed in the rhythms of sowing and planting. It can be suggested to the parents that they plant a small garden on the grave with bulbs that will flower in springtime.

6. Funerals

Funeral practices vary from one culture to another. The Christian dimension of such rituals should emphasize the link with baptism. The following texts and symbols could be used in vigils for the deceased at home or in hospital or during the reception of the bodily remains in a church. Such vigils do not necessarily need the involvement of an ordained minister.

Leader: It is in baptism that we enter eternal life. It is God's gift to us through water and the Holy Spirit that we are reborn into everlasting life. Let us think again about the meaning of our baptism.

• *The Paschal Candle*
Attention can be drawn to the paschal candle.

When God created the world there was darkness over the deep, and God's Spirit hovered over the chaos. God said, "Let there be light" and there was light. God saw that the light was good. The early Christians spoke of Jesus as the light that had come into the world, and so they gathered in the evening darkness to commemorate his life. And then they lit a candle to celebrate his presence among them. *(Pause)*

When N. was baptized he/she received the light of Christ. N. was asked to keep the flame of faith alive until the Lord comes. Then he/she would meet him with all the saints of the heavenly kingdom.

• *Water*
A jug and bowl of water can be used to focus on the blessed water.

Christ says: Let everyone who listens answer, "Come." Then let all who are thirsty come: all who want it may have the water of life, and have it free. As the Jews of old were led to new life through the waters of the Red Sea may N. be led from us to the water of new life.

(Pause)

N. was brought to the waters of baptism as an infant. May all who are buried with Christ in the death of baptism also rise with him to newness of life.

• *Oil*

A small bowl of oil can be used here.

One of the great gifts of God's creation is fruit-bearing trees. From the fruit of the olive tree oil is pressed. In the Old Testament, people were anointed with oil to make them sacred. Of old the Jews spoke of David as God's anointed, the one set apart to be their king. The early Christians spoke of Jesus as the new David, and so they called him Christ, which means "the anointed one."

(Pause)

In baptism N. was anointed with the chrism of salvation and welcomed into God's holy people. Just as Christ was anointed priest, prophet, and king, N. was born into Christ's body in order to share in the wonder of everlasting life. May the oils of our baptism strengthen us today in the face of sorrow and loss.

The following text might be read. Two readers are required.

1. Our hearts are heavy at the loss of N.
2. Come to me all you who labor and are overburdened, and I will give you rest. Shoulder my yoke and learn from me, for I am gentle and humble in heart and you will find rest for your souls. Yes, my yoke is easy and my burden light.

1. Naturally we ask at this time, why do people die?
2. Unless a wheat grain falls on the ground and dies, it remains only a single grain; but if it dies it yields a rich harvest.

1. It is hard to believe that N., who has died, will live forever.
2. I am the resurrection. If anyone believes in me, even though he dies he will live, and whoever lives and believes in me will never die.

1. We pray today in hope that N., who has died, is at peace.
2. Only in God is my soul at rest, from him comes my hope. He alone is my rock, my fortress. Unburden your hearts onto him for God is our shelter.

1. It is difficult to understand why our family and friends must die.
2. St. Paul says that God's foolishness is wiser than human wisdom and God's weakness is stronger than human strength. It is when I am weak that I am strong, for I feel the power of Christ shining through my human weakness.

1. We do not know what the future holds for those who have died but we trust in God's promise.
2. May the choirs of angels welcome you and lead you to Abraham's side. Where Lazarus is poor no longer, may you have eternal rest.

Appendix

Texts for use in rituals

1. Letting go

This text should simply be read reflectively by one reader.

Lord God help me to let go.
Life is an endless process of letting go;
In our birth we had to let go of the security
of our mother's womb and emerge into a strange world;
In adolescence we let go of the innocence of childhood;
All of us have to let go of home: parents must let go of their
children, and children must let go of their parents;
Throughout life as we grow and mature we must continually
let go of opinions, jobs, good health, and ultimately of the idea
that we are in control.
And, of course, in death we must let go of those we love.
Between womb and tomb life is an endless process
of letting go.
Come, Holy Spirit, help me to let go so that even when the letting go is tearful and sad it will awaken me to the mystery and
wonder of life.
Life is the greatest gift we have received, and we must, in the
end, let go of this gift.
We must let go of the past to let God
be the God of the future.

2. Fear

*Each line begins with "I am," "you are" or "we are." This text is
particularly suitable when read along with Ecclesiastes 3:1–8.*

For adults:
You are not afraid of dying to the old.
You are not afraid of giving birth to what is new.
You are not afraid of planting.
You are not afraid of uprooting what has been planted.
You are not afraid of searching.
You are not afraid of keeping or throwing away.
You are not afraid of tears or mourning.
You are not afraid of laughter.

For adolescents:
You are not afraid of dying to childhood ways.
You are not afraid of giving birth to wisdom and courage.
You are not afraid of planting responsibility in your life.
You are not afraid of uprooting what needs to be changed.
You are not afraid of searching for the man/woman
that is within you.
You are not afraid of becoming independent and free.
You are not afraid of mourning your break with the past.
You are not afraid of embracing the future.

3. I am

This text should simply be read reflectively by one reader.

I am the wind of the sea,
I am the wave of the ocean,
I am the wind that blows,
I am the fire that burns.

I am not afraid of dying,
I am not afraid of searching,
I have gone where I would rather not go,
I have drunk from the water of life.

4. The power of Paul's words

There should be two readers reciting the texts alternately with a short pause between each one. Ideally the two readers should stand at lecterns at opposite ends of the relevant space.

1. The word of God cuts more finely than a double-edged sword. It cuts between the marrow and the bone so that the truth can emerge.
2. What we preach is Christ crucified; a scandal for Jews and folly for Greeks, but for us, who believe, the wisdom and the glory of God. For God's foolishness is wiser than human wisdom, and God's weakness is stronger than human strength.

1. It is when I am weak that I am strong, for I feel the power of Christ shining through my human weakness.
2. I, Paul, appointed by God to be an apostle, send greetings to the church of God in Corinth, to the holy people of Jesus Christ who are called to take their place among all the saints everywhere. May God our Father and the Lord Jesus Christ send you grace and peace.

1. Nothing can ever come between us and the love of God made visible in Christ Jesus our Lord. No angel, no power, no division, no fear can ever separate us from the love of God.
2. The blessing cup that we bless is a communion with the blood of Christ, and the bread that we break is a communion with the body of Christ. Because there is only one loaf means that we, though many, are one body because we all share the one loaf and the one cup.

1. Love is always patient and kind, it is never jealous. Love is never boastful or conceited, it is never rude or selfish. Love takes no pleasure in other people's sins but delights in the truth. It is always ready to excuse, to trust, to hope, and to endure whatever comes.

2. Are you people in Galatia mad? Are you going to surrender the power of the Spirit and become slaves again? Surely you realize that Christ died for you and that you are now free?

1. We are only earthenware jars that hold this treasure, to make it clear that such an overwhelming power comes from God and not from us. We are in difficulties on all sides but never fear; we see no answer to our problems but never despair.

2. I thank my God each time I think of you, and every time I pray for you, I pray with joy.

5. The spirit of God and the spirit of the world

Two readers are needed: one reads the spirit of the world and the other the spirit of God. In each case the spirit of the world comes first followed within a couple of seconds by the spirit of God; there is then a substantial pause (10-15 seconds) before moving on. Ideally the two readers should stand at lecterns at opposite ends of the relevant space.

1. The spirit of the world says that externals are all important—looks, property, possessions. We are what we have.
2. The spirit of God says that our looks and appearance can be very deceptive. We must look into the heart, into the depth of life to see who we really are.

1. The spirit of the world says that life is a test, and success is everything. It abhors failure and disappointment.
2. The spirit of God says that failure can be more important than success. We can learn much even from the sad and more difficult times.

1. The spirit of the world says that the great problems—unemployment, ecology, violence—have nothing to do with us. We've just got to mind our own business.
2. The spirit of God says that we am responsible for everyone, everywhere, at all times. There are no strangers in God's eyes.

1. The spirit of the world says that love is about things going well, in accord with our plans.
2. The spirit of God says that love is about giving of ourselves, even when we feel that we cannot.

1. The spirit of the world says that there is no such thing as forgiveness because there is no such thing as sin.
2. The spirit of God says that forgiveness is the greatest reality that we know. We sin, we fail, yet we can be freed to go on.

1. The spirit of the world says that honesty and commitment are impossible and don't really exist.
2. The spirit of God says that honesty and commitment are the only things that really matter in the end.

1. The spirit of the world says that the sick and the disabled are not really alive. Sickness and disability are disastrous.
2. The spirit of God says that the sick and the disabled are often those who are most alive for they know their dependence; they know that life is not in their control.

1. The spirit of the world says that death is the end of life and proves that life is futile.
2. The spirit of God says that death is not the end of life because the great spirit present in us is not extinguished but transformed.

6. The community of Pentecost

This text can be read by one or more readers.

Remember the famous scene in the upper room when the disciples and Mary were waiting for the gift of the Spirit. Did you ever think much about the reality that they faced? In many ways that group, which included Mary the Mother of Jesus, was very akin to our gathering here today.

Some people in the upper room were doubtful about what it was all about; similarly some of us here are doubtful, wondering if we should be here at all.

Some were enthusiastic, bursting to tell the message to others; undoubtedly some of us are enthusiastic to get out there and tell people the good news.

Some of the disciples were very confused by everything that had happened to them; some of us are very confused by what has happened to us in our lives.

Some of the folk had grown cynical about the whole thing, believing that they had been fooled; maybe some of us have grown cynical too, having seen so much that disheartens us in the church and in religion in general.

Some of the disciples were broken by all the suffering and death they had witnessed; some of us are broken by life, by illness, by death.

Others of the disciples were worried and didn't know where to turn; some of us carry great worries about what the future holds.

Presumably some of the people in the upper room were bored, wondering if anything was ever going to happen; some of us probably find life tedious and wonder if it has any value.

And finally there were those who were deeply hopeful in the

midst of it all, trusting in God's promise; equally there are people of deep hope and joy sitting in our midst today.

So if you count yourself somewhere, anywhere, among those who are doubtful, enthusiastic, confused, cynical, broken, worried, bored, hopeful, or joyful, then take great heart, for it was to such as these that the Spirit of God was first given. It was to a motley crew like ourselves that God gave the greatest gift: not to those who had all the answers, or to those who had life all sewn up, but rather to those who were struggling with the realities of life.

Note: instead of saying "some of us" or "some people" in the second phrase, one could say, "all of us at times are...."

7. My story with biblical eyes

In each case a personal reflection comes first followed after a pause by a biblical quotation; there is then a further pause before moving on. Ideally the two readers should stand at lecterns at opposite ends of the relevant space.

1. We are children of the earth, made of the same stuff as the stars; we are part of the beauty of the earth.
2. In the beginning God created the heavens and the earth. Now the earth was a formless void, there was darkness over the deep, and God's Spirit hovered over the water. God saw what God had made and it was very good.

1. Think of the date you were born, the joy of your parents, family, neighbors and friends. Imagine yourself as a baby.
2. Before I formed you in the womb I knew you, before you came to birth I consecrated you.

1. Recall in your own mind the various places you've lived. Think of the houses, the places—go into each of them in your mind.
2. Wherever you go, I will go, wherever you live I will live.

1. Think of a couple of really happy moments in your life. Treasure them in your heart.
2. I want you to be happy, always happy in the Lord; I repeat, what I want is your happiness.

1. Allow moments of suffering and pain to enter your mind. They are part of who we are.
2. Come to me all you who labor and are overburdened and I will give you rest. For my yoke is easy and my burden is light.

1. Who are the people who accompany you? family, spouse, children, neighbors, friends? Look at their faces now.
2. Did not our hearts burn within us as he talked to us on the road and explained the Scriptures to us...and their eyes

were opened and they recognized him in the breaking of
the bread.

1. What do you hope for? What are your greatest expectations, your cherished dreams?
2. What we suffer in this life can never be compared to the
   glory that is yet to be revealed.

1. Where will it all end? What will happen in the future?
2. I saw a new heaven and a new earth.... Then I heard a loud
   voice call from above: now I am making the whole of creation new.

8. A blessing on leaving a Christian gathering

This text should simply be read reflectively by one reader.

You are the salt of the earth,
you are the light of the world,
together we are the body of Christ.
As a baby you were baptized in Christ,
at seven years you were invited to eat from the altar of God,
and later the church confirmed the gift of God's Spirit
given to you.
Go now from this holy place,
treasure in your heart the wonder of who you are,
and may the words you have heard here ever echo
in your mind.
You are the salt of the earth,
you are the light of the world,
together we are the body of Christ.

9. Take, bless, break, and give

This text should simply be read reflectively by one reader.

In the Eucharist bread is taken, blessed, broken, and given.
In life we are taken, blessed, broken, and given.
The priest takes the bread in his hands and blesses it during
the eucharistic prayer;
then he breaks it, and it is given to us as the body of Christ.
Through our birth and baptism we are taken into God's hands;
as the bread is taken, so too are we.
In life we are blessed by family, friends, love, and joy;
as the bread is blessed, so too are we.
We are broken by failure, sin, pain, and heartbreak;
as the bread is broken, so too are we.
In death we are given back to the mystery
from which we came;
as the bread is given, so too are we.
When we take, bless, break, and give bread to one another,
we believe the Lord to be especially present in our midst.
But we must learn to accept that in his memory
we will be taken, blessed, broken, and given
for the life of the world.

10. Renewal of baptismal promises

Leader: Do you believe in God the creator of light and darkness, land and sea, heaven and earth, woman and man?
All: We do.

Leader: Do you cherish and protect the earth as God's creation?
All: We do.

Leader: Do you appreciate the gift of water that endlessly renews and sustains life?
All: We do.

Leader: Do you give thanks for the spring and the summer, the
sowing and the harvest, the sun and the moon, the wind
and the rain, the mountaintop, and the seashore?
All: We do.

Leader: Do you believe that in the midst of a beautiful world we,
like Adam and Eve, live in the shadow of temptation and evil?
All: We do.

Leader: Do you reject all that is evil?
All: We do.

Leader: Do you reject injustice, hatred, despair, and bigotry?
All: We do.

Leader: Do you reject all that undermines and destroys the gift
of life?
All: We do.

Leader: Do you believe that Jesus Christ is the Savior of the
world?
All: We do.

Leader: Do you believe that Jesus died for us on Calvary and
was raised from the dead?
All: We do.

Leader: Do you believe that in baptism you became followers
of Jesus?

All: We do.

Leader: Do you believe that when you were anointed with oil in baptism you received the gift of God's Spirit?
All: We do.

Leader: Do you believe that God's Spirit is present in humanity and that our destiny is to share fully in God's own life?
All: We do.

Leader: Do you accept the Christian identity that was given to you in your name at baptism?
All: We do.

Leader: Do you accept that your faith can only be lived with others in a Christian community?
All: We do.

Leader: Do you believe that the church, a community of saints and sinners, is the temple of God's presence in the world?
All: We do.

Leader: Do you take responsibility for the future well-being of the church?
All: We do.

Leader: Do you believe in the final triumph of Christ over sin, light over darkness, truth over lies, hope over despair, good over evil, and life over death?
All: We do.

Leader: Do you today, in the presence of fellow believers, confirm the meaning and implications of your baptism?
All: We do.

Leader: Do you now promise to live your life in accordance with the Christian faith, which we have professed together?
All: We do.

Leader: Then may God bless you and strengthen you as you bear witness to your faith.

11. Peter's faith (according to John's Gospel)

Three readers are required. This text can simply be read reflectively or acted out as a role play.

Voice 1: In the evening of the first day of the week, Jesus showed himself to his disciples. He turned to Simon Peter and said: "Simon, son of John, do you love me?"

Voice 2: Yes, Lord, you know I love you.

Voice 3: While Simon Peter and another disciple were standing outside the door of the high priest's house, the woman keeping the door said to him, "aren't you one of that man's disciples?"

Voice 2: I am not.

Voice 1: Jesus asked again: "Simon, son of John, do you love me?"

Voice 2: Yes, Lord, you know I love you.

Voice 3: One of the servants turned to Peter and said: "You are one of his disciples surely; didn't I see you with him?"

Voice 2: I tell you I do not know the man.

Voice 1: A third time Jesus said: "Simon, son of John, do you love me?"

Voice 2: Yes, Lord, you know all things, you know I love you.

Voice 3: A woman standing by the fire turned to Peter and said: "You are one of his disciples. Why, you are a Galilean! Your accent gives you away."

Voice 2: I tell you I don't know what you are talking about. I swear I never saw the man.

Voice 1: You are Peter and upon this rock I will build my church. Feed my lambs. Feed my sheep.

12. Affirming the Christian commitment of women

Two readers are required.

First voice: Ruth's mother-in-law was called Naomi and she had
lost both her sons. In desperation and loneliness she decided
to return to her homeland. She told Ruth that she had no
more sons and that life with her had no future. However
Ruth did not desert her mother-in-law. She said to her:
"Wherever you go I will go, wherever you live I will live."
Pause
May you, like Ruth, be blessed with faithfulness and
perseverance. As pilgrims on the journey of life, may you
remain steadfast in your faith even in the midst of disillu-
sionment and disappointment.

Second voice: After the resurrection, and while the followers of
Jesus cowered in despair and fear, Mary of Magdala set out
to tend the body of Jesus. Through this act of courage she
became the first person to encounter the risen Christ. Jesus
then sent this woman to bring the good news to the others.
Pause
As women in the church, may you show leadership in the
face of doubt and dejection. Continue to believe in the
promises of Christ so that you may be a wellspring of healing and hope in a broken world.

First voice: Mary as a young mother said "yes" to the will of
God. She nurtured the divine in the human and in her
womb bore God to the world. Mary followed her son all the
way to the cross.
Pause
As women in the church, say "yes" to God's word and nurture the divine presence in the human. As mothers, build a
church that is home to all.

13. Affirming the Christian commitment of men

Two readers are required.

First voice: As a young man Jeremiah was told by God "before I formed you in the womb I knew you, before you came to birth I consecrated you." Jeremiah was consecrated as a prophet and became a man who courageously spoke the truth. Many did not want to hear what he said because he condemned the wrongdoer and gave hope to the outcast.

Pause

Second voice: As men, the world tells you to be powerful, to accumulate wealth and popularity. It tells you to be successful, to do well for yourself. May you be blessed like Jeremiah as prophet and speaker of the truth. Tell the world that the voice of the Spirit says be charitable, be merciful, forgive those who wrong you, and be honest and just in your dealings always.

First voice: When the Hebrews were slaves in Egypt they cried out to God to free them. God called Moses to liberate his people. He used no weapons, had no army, yet the spirit of the warrior within him fought and challenged the powers that held the people in bondage. God blessed the courage of this man and empowered him to lead the Hebrews through the waters of the Red Sea and into freedom.

Pause

Second voice: May God bless you with a brave heart to fight for the liberation of men and women from the oppression of injustice and despair.

First voice: John the Baptist wore a garment of camel skin, and he lived on locusts and wild honey. His home was the wilderness, and his work was to preach repentance and to baptize in the waters of the Jordan. He was an outcast and lived alone, yet this man prepared the way for the Lord. It was this wild man that announced the coming of Christ into the world.

Pause

As men, may you find within yourselves the energy and courage to speak about Christ and prepare a way for his message in your homes, your places of work and in your communities.

14. Affirming the Christian commitment of the ordained

Two readers are required.

First voice: The name Abraham means Great Father. He was a
  man who had to leave his family, his father's house, and his
  country to go to the land that God had shown him. He was
  to become the greatest of pilgrims. God blessed him and
  made of him a great nation.

Pause

Second voice: As a priest, you too have sacrificed the comforts
  of home in order to lead your people as pilgrims on a spiritual journey. May God bless you and your work.

First voice: Solomon was consecrated king of his people. God
  offered him any gift that he wanted. He asked for a heart to
  govern his people and to know right from wrong.

Pause

Second voice: We pray that, like Solomon, people will say of you:
  You give justice to the poor.
  You save children from poverty.
  You free the lowly and helpless who call on you.
  You take pity on the poor and weak.
  And the souls of the powerless you save
  for they are precious in your eyes. *(see Psalm 72:4, 12–4)*

First voice: Paul who once zealously persecuted Christians was
  filled with the spirit of God to courageously preach Christ
  crucified. In the infancy of the church he formed communities of service and provided leadership to those who were
  lost and downhearted.

Pause

Second voice: As priests, do all you can to preserve the unity of
  your communities. Bring reconciliation where there is divi-

sion, comfort where there is loss, and hope where there is despair. And glory be to God whose power working in you can do infinitely more than you can ask or even imagine.

15. Examination of Conscience

Two readers are required.

Voice 1: Bless me, Father, for I have sinned; it is three weeks since my last confession.

Voice 2: It might be a month, a year, ten years, but we all need to speak about our real problems, our fears, our real failures. There is nothing worse in life than carrying great burdens for years. We need to be released, to be healed, to be forgiven.

Voice 1: I cursed.

Voice 2: Yes, I use some bad language but that is not cursing in the true sense. To curse is the opposite of to praise. We should give praise and thanks at all times; praise God for the wonder of creation; thank God and our forebears for the gift of life; dance for joy before the rainbow, the sea, the sky and the stars. But instead I find myself cursing my luck, and I forget to give praise and thanks.

Voice 1: I stole.

Voice 2: I've never really stolen anything significant, or have I? I suppose that I've often stolen the wonder from people's lives by my moodiness. I've stolen others' dignity by refusing to acknowledge their value, their independence. I've stolen my own beauty by not treasuring the gift of my own life.

Voice 1: I didn't say my prayers.

Voice 2: Usually I just forget them. I remember to pray when I need something or I am stuck in a rut. Now that I have some time to think, I should reflect about things. I have family and friends. My table is bountiful and my home warm. I can see the sunrise and the sunset, and I can hear the wind and the rain. I am alive. In my ordinary life, however, I tend to forget these things. To pray is to truly remember.

Voice 1: I lied.

Voice 2: We all tell the odd white lie. Yet it's easy to get into the habit of lying. I lie when I fail to see the truth in another person. The truth is that everyone is precious in God's eyes. Do I ever ask myself whether what I've heard is true or not? To only speak the truth is difficult and demanding.

Voice 1: I missed Mass.

Voice 2: I know I should go because it's an obligation. But it can be very tedious and repetitive, and I am easily distracted. Yet I am part of the great story that is being told. When the bread is broken, so too I experience brokenness and difficulty. When the wine is poured, so too am I asked to give of myself to the rest of the world. When the community gathered I wasn't present. I missed Mass and missed out on part of who I am.

16. A Blessing on Getting Married

This text should be read reflectively by one reader.

May you know joy in each other's company,
and may your love carry you through the years ahead.

May your friends be plentiful and your table bountiful,
and may God's face smile upon your home.

May laughter and pleasure be with you always,
and may you grow old in the warmth of your embrace.

May compassion and understanding accompany you,
and through forgiveness may your love turn to gold.

17. Prayer of a newly married couple

The couple could read this text together, or each person might read
alternate verses.

We give thanks for our parents
and for the gift of life;
for their sacrifice,
protection, and a thousand hugs.

We give thanks for our family,
for fights and forgiveness,
for memories, too many to mention,
and presents at Christmastime.

We give thanks for our friends,
for generosity and loyalty,
for laughter and sorrow,
and secrets kept.

We give thanks to God
for the waters of baptism;
for Jesus' self-sacrifice
and the Spirit of love.

In thanksgiving, we pray that we may be
as generous and as kind as you are.
And may our marriage strengthen us all the days of our life
to be truly Christian in faith, hope, and love.

18. A mother's prayer on the death of her child

The context will determine how best to use a text like this.

The land of our promise was populated with every kind of
hope for you,
every kind of wish for your life.
We had imagined who you would be like;
handsome and witty, thought your father,
practical and purposeful like your mother, I claimed.
Little child, why did you go away
before you had learned to live at all?

They said you'd keep us up all night,
that things would never be the same again.
Friends hoped to see your father with a diaper in his hand,
with tired eyes and a sleepy head.
The fun we'd have putting you to bed.
Little child, you have turned our world upside down,
our tired eyes and our sleepy heads.

Your father enthused about the talents on his side of the family.
You'd be a professional, a doctor most likely!
I wondered what your ways would be like;
would you be grumpy like your grandfather,
or mellow and secretive like grandma?
The questions and questions that go 'round in my mind.

You are a mystery and a feast of answers,
an unknown martyr, and an innocent victim
of the dark and terrible ways of this world.
One day this veil of mourning will be lifted
and we will be with you where you are now going.
Be there, N., to put your arms around us,
For in you, little child, we have seen a glimpse of heaven.

19. Reflecting on death

Two readers are required.

1. Our hearts are heavy at the loss of N.

2. Come to me all you who labor and are overburdened, and I will give you rest. Shoulder my yoke and learn from me, for I am gentle and humble in heart and you will find rest for your souls. Yes, my yoke is easy and my burden light.

1. Naturally we ask at this time, why do people die?

2. Unless a wheat grain falls on the ground and dies, it remains only a single grain; but if it dies it yields a rich harvest.

1. It is hard to believe that N., who has died, will live forever.

2. I am the resurrection. If anyone believes in me, even though he dies he will live, and whoever lives and believes in me will never die.

1. We pray today in hope that N., who has died, is at peace.

2. Only in God is my soul at rest, from him comes my hope. He alone is my rock, my fortress. Unburden your hearts onto him for God is our shelter.

1. It is difficult to understand why our family and friends must die.

2. St. Paul says that God's foolishness is wiser than human wisdom and God's weakness is stronger than human strength. It is when I am weak that I am strong, for I feel the power of Christ shining through my human weakness.

1. We do not know what the future holds for those who have died, but we trust in God's promise.

2. May the choirs of angels welcome you and lead you to Abraham's side. Where Lazarus is poor no longer, may you have eternal rest.